Psychology and Capitalism

The Manipulation of Mind

Psychology and Capitalism

The Manipulation of Mind

Ron Roberts

Winchester, UK
Washington, USA

First published by Zero Books, 2015
Zero Books is an imprint of John Hunt Publishing Ltd., Laurel House, Station Approach,
Alresford, Hants, SO24 9JH, UK
office1@jhpbooks.net
www.johnhuntpublishing.com
www.zero-books.net

For distributor details and how to order please visit the 'Ordering' section on our website.

Text copyright: Ron Roberts 2014

ISBN: 978 1 78279 654 1

All rights reserved. Except for brief quotations in critical articles or reviews, no part of this
book may be reproduced in any manner without prior written permission from the publishers.

The rights of Ron Roberts as author have been asserted in accordance with the Copyright,
Designs and Patents Act 1988.

A CIP catalogue record for this book is available from the British Library.

Design: Lee Nash

Printed and bound by CPI Group (UK) Ltd, Croydon, CR0 4YY

We operate a distinctive and ethical publishing philosophy in all
areas of our business, from our global network of authors to
production and worldwide distribution.

CONTENTS

Man knows himself only as much as he knows the world.
Johann Wolfgang von Goethe

Turning economic contradictions into psychological problems is one of the standard tricks of bourgeois ideology.
Lucien Sève

We're all living in Amerika.
Rammstein

For Svetlana

Acknowledgements

My thanks as ever to all those who have contributed to the ideas in this book, either through discussion, shared experience or intellectual/practical endeavour. In particular I would like to extend warm thanks to Merry for her continued support over many years and to Svetlana for wonderful conversation and company and for enabling me to see both psychology and London in a different light.

Chapter I

Origins: A Dangerous Science

Control, in any complete sense, is not an aim but a dangerous myth.
(Bannister & Fransella, 1971, p.201)

Origins

If we are to fully consider the central thesis of this book – that the nature of psychology as an academic discipline is inextricably bound up with the character of the socio-economic and political realm – we must of necessity examine the historical contexts within which it first arose and then subsequently developed. An inspection of any number of textbooks places the emergence of scientific psychology in the second half of the 19th century. This was when Wilhelm Wundt, working at Leipzig University, set up the first laboratory of experimental psychology. His aim was to establish a new domain of science fused from earlier philo-sophical studies of mind and an experimental tradition borrowed from physiology, which had investigated the body as a purely mechanical system. Wundt wished his experimental psychology to bridge the gap between the investigation of physi-ological processes and what could be revealed through intro-spection – the process of examining one's own conscious thoughts and feelings. In this Wundt was monumentally unsuc-cessful.

However, to begin the story from Wundt is already too late. Accounts of the history of experimental psychology which do so fall into the trap of uncritically accepting psychology's claims that its experimental tradition was a logical extension of Enlightenment thought. The Enlightenment was a cultural movement which swept across Europe in the 17th and 18th centuries aiming to not only revolutionise thought but change society through the force of reason, argument and evidence alone. What psychology claims in effect is that its growth and influence stem from the scientific and intellectual strength alone of its arguments, and not the touch nor the influence of politics, power, privileged interest, money or emotion. This was an account which American textbook writers at the end of the 19th century wished to promote, but it was far from the truth.

Psychology's real history began a good 300 years prior to Wundt's appearance on the scene. Before 1500 there was no mention in any literature of the word psychology; its first recorded use was by the Croatian humanist and Latinist Marko Marulić in his book, *Psichiologia de ratione animae humanae* in the late 15th or early 16th century. Its first use in the English language was by Steven Blankaart in 1694 in *The Physical Dictionary* which refers to "Anatomy, which treats of the Body, and Psychology, which treats of the Soul" (cited in Itten & Roberts, 2014, p.61). A real danger in linking early use of the term to its present application lies in assuming that the terms are addressing the same phenomenon. While Newton's treatment of gravity in the 17th century and Einstein's in the 20th century are clearly different, they are dealing with the same phenomenon – the actions of free-falling bodies in a gravitational field, and the nature of the attractive force between them. In psychology's case, however, we have to tread carefully. As can be seen from its early use, the word pertains to the soul, a non-material presumed entity whose existence few if any psychologists or psychotherapists of the 21st century would subscribe to. An even greater danger is to project contemporary psychological terms back in historical time and make presumptions about both the way people experienced the world and the value of contemporary hypothesised psychological constructs in explaining how they behaved in it.

In fact not long after psychology entered the lexicon, the noted philosopher Immanuel Kant dismissed the possibility of psychology as a natural science. The best it could hope for, he argued, given that psychology lacked any axiomatic basis (a system of undisputed *a priori* propositions from which to proceed), as well as the considerable problems associated with introspection, was to proceed empirically and produce a collection of facts which could be ordered and classified. As such it would at best comprise an historical doctrine of nature (Brysbaert & Rastle, 2013). This criticism finds echoes in Kenneth Gergen's (1973) argument, toward the end of the 20th century, that psychology is not a science and should be considered a branch of historical knowledge, capable only of statements whose truths are contingent on time and place (see Chapter 2). Kant queried the value of introspection – the attempt to systematically make observations of one's own mind – because not only does one alter, by observing, what is being observed, but what is doing the observing and what is being observed are one and the same. Karl Popper's view of science was that it needs "points of view and theoretical problems" (2002, p.88). Psychology, when it began, had neither. Arguably this is still the case.

Auguste Comte, the founder of sociology as well as the doctrine of positivism, made similar arguments. To him psychology's subject matter, the soul, was beyond the reach of the senses and immeasurable. It could never attain the status of a science. Notwithstanding these objections, psychology developed initially as a branch of philosophy (Intellectual philosophy) considering the various products of the mind – such as dreams, thoughts, ideas, emotions, imagination, will and moral reasoning. The first textbooks of psychology duly began to appear around the late 18th and early 19th centuries. The fledgling attempts to establish psychology as a coherent discipline were met with widespread scepticism as to its possible utility. The first steps to rebrand psychology as an experimental social science began in earnest with Wundt's aforementioned use of introspection in 1879. Wundt's work, though oft cited as the celebrated first use of the experimental method in the nascent discipline, actually yielded little by way of fruitful knowledge. For psychology to be given the kick start into respectability, developments outside the disciple were what came to have the greatest influence in both shaping what went on (and still goes on) within it and in determining its practical utility. It was Kant's suggestion that psychology could only usefully proceed through classification and ordering that proved the more prescient and led to psychology finding or inventing something which it could measure.

Historical, Political and Technological Influences

The key developments for psychology as a discipline were historical, political, cultural, social and technical. Christianity and the Protestant reformation in particular had paved the way for a form of individualism to develop. Stressing one's private relationship with God, Christianity's influence was multiplied by a series of technological developments. These included not only the mirror – which perforce encouraged and increased self-awareness – but also the printing press, which in turn led to more widespread literacy, letter-writing and the birth of the novel. On top of these the feudal order was giving way to the new capitalist one which led to the new mercantile capitalist class promoting the private accumulation of capital and wealth above the collective ownership and use of natural resources. The early period of industrialisation saw marked increases in the human population and the rapid rise of industrial centres of production to which people from the country flocked. With rapid urban growth there were an entirely new series of problems about how power and control were to be maintained. The ruling class of the day sought to exert this control through gathering ever more information about the hordes of people who not only were occupying the new urban spaces but also constituted the producers of the various forms of new wealth through their labour. As the divisions of labour multiplied, it became increas-

4

ingly important to be able to categorise this potential workforce in terms of who could and couldn't do what kind of work.

Classification, Statistics, Norms and Deviance

It was thus in the 18th century and the beginning of the industrial revolution that psychology got its modern impetus. The young discipline, as yet lacking any demonstrable utility, was able to acquire it through the help of another new discipline then pushing out its first shoots above the soil of the new social order. That discipline was statistics. The impetus behind its foundation was to construct a science of the state – hence its name. The young science of the state initially concerned itself with collecting demographic and economic data. Accordingly it became known as *Political Arithmetic* in English, and later took its name from the German *Statistik*. Here begins the numerical disciplining of people and the social spaces they inhabit into various boxes, categories and packages.

The centuries-long process of surveillance effectively began here and runs all the way to the modern security state. Despite the almost ubiquitous presence of statistics in contemporary psychology, it is imperative to stress that it began not to enhance human well-being or to promote a deeper understanding of the natural world, but to serve the needs of government and central administrative bodies. Without an awareness of this, one cannot fully appreciate psychology's preoccupation with coding, counting and classifying people – i.e. turning them into numbers outside of this history. Neither can one understand the long history of surveillance – that directly authorised by the state or that internally practiced on oneself – without contemplating how statistics contributes to it. The development of statistics as a discipline leads to normative descriptions of human beings and human social groups – height, weight, family size, age etc. Only in the 19th century did statistics escape this enclave to become a general method of analysis and interpretation of data.

One of the troubles with statistical norms is that from being purely descriptive their use can shift imperceptibly to being prescriptive – used as a basis for saying not how things are but how they should be. A recurrent feature of the use of so-called psychological norms is that the descriptive aspect rapidly disappears and all that is left is the prescriptive, mystifyingly announced as 'value free' science. This is how we come to mistakenly accept social norms of behaviour as prescriptions for how we ought to behave, even in the absence of information as to how people do behave in actual real-world situations. Human situations of course, without fail, unfold in historical contexts – one reason why they are poorly understood. In reality the enormous variety of possible situations coupled with the clash of people's unknown histories means that a prescriptive account of how people ought to be expected to behave based on prior probability cannot be known. On top of this, mere facts can never logically give rise to statements regarding what ought to be. Ifs do not lead to shoulds. These are arrived at outside the scientific arena and then imported into it by a system of smoke and mirrors to claim scientific backing for what are essentially political or moral judgments. One of the few psychologists to come clean on this is Marie Jahoda, who in a foreword to Laing, Phillipson and Lee's *Interpersonal Perception* admitted that there can be "no norms for interpersonal encounters" (1966, p.iv) – a piece of wisdom that, sadly never made it out of the 1960s.

As political arithmetic developed, what could not escape the attention of the administrative class during this period of social transition was the large numbers of people who, from the point of view of the state – a state run naturally enough by the wealthy for the wealthy – served no useful economic function, and disrupted the day to day lives of those who did. These comprised an assortment of beggars, prostitutes, criminals, the sick, the disabled and the mad, as well as those whose personal conduct was embarrassing to the reputation of their wealthy relatives. The sheer numbers of such people meant that the powerful of the day were motivated to do something. What had begun in England as a relatively small-scale operation, the parking of one's 'aberrant' relatives in a madhouse, eventually increased in scale. What began with private madhouses – usually very small establishments catering for only a handful of individuals and, initially, run by the clergy – came to be run-for-profit businesses led by the burgeoning medical profession seeking to expand their sphere of influence. This they did as religious influence waned. A veritable 'trade in lunacy' ensued. The presence of doctors lent credence to the claims they advanced that those of unsound mind were not simply unruly but ill. Even then however the legitimacy of the 'alienists,' as the mad-doctors came to be known, was widely questioned – even from within the medical profession.

Madness, Distress and Social Control

Eventually as the power of the nation states increased, large-scale asylums for the insane sprang up, housing mainly poor people. By 1800, there were around 5000 people in England confined in these asylums, out of a population of 10 million (Cromby, Harper & Reavey, 2013). The aim of these early mental hospitals was social reform not healing. And within the mantle of social reform lurked the shadow of social control. Around this time a new 'moral' treatment for the inmates of asylums became fashionable throughout Europe and the United States, challenging the biological stance of medicine. Its chief protagonist, Pinel, while scathing about the coercive conduct of doctors – "the doctrine of superior force," he wrote, "is not less applicable to the practice of medicine, than to the science of politics" (cited in Read, 2004, p.18) – was also frank that he himself was trying to impose society's moral code on 'deviant' individuals. He particularly wished to eradicate what he saw as celibacy, promiscuity, apathy and laziness and to do this by

7

having his charges internalise authority to police their own behaviour. The purveyors of moral management however lacked any institutional power-base and so medicine eventually reasserted its authority, professionalised the asylums and imposed a biological dogma on public understanding of the people imprisoned there. Not all agreed.

The management of madness and psychological distress is pivotal to the establishment of psychiatry as a social force and arguably also central to its development along with that of psychology. The continuing popularity of psychology is fed in part by a desire amongst its followers – students, academics and therapists – that it will somehow deliver to them knowledge of how to live a better life and escape from the pitfalls of the psychological pains they (and we) all endure. This is a seriously misplaced wish. The major influences on our lives we believe are those we can most easily see – emanating from one's friends, lovers, family and associates. But the larger more powerful forces in society lie unseen and remote and forever untheorised by psychologists.

Madness, symbolically at least, points to something beyond our understanding – an invitation to another more frightening world than the one we know. The attraction of the arts of psychiatry and psychology for students and state alike is to tame this beast and thereby gain power over the terrible unknown. The apparent absence of reason to be found in the mad serves to strengthen and legitimise the importance which the Enlightenment has given to it and to which the young disciplines of psychology and psychiatry have hitched a ride. The myth of reason as the cure for all ills was a child of the Enlightenment and once unleashed knew no bounds. Its corresponding dark side is the fear of insanity. Goya's famous etching, created as the 18th century drew to a close – "The Sleep of Reason Produces Monsters" – expresses this fear in a nightmarish vision. Writing in the mid-19th century Marx saw the increasing lunatic population as a direct consequence of capitalism. But this was a view from the fringe. With medicine firmly in the ascendency, Marx's view would sink almost without trace.

Measurement and Inheritance

The medicalisation of madness contributed two of the key pillars of thought which were to play an important role in securing the 'scientific' credentials of psychology. Chief amongst these was the viability of diagnosing, classifying and categorizing troublesome people. This penchant for labelling and pigeon-holing people via the use of scientific-sounding labels – preferably with Latin or Greek etymology – fed off the lure of Enlightenment thinking and was taken up with gusto by the new psychoanalytic movement led by Freud at the end of the 19th century. The view that Freud helped promulgate, that mental illness was ubiquitous (nobody was exempt), has obviously been of seminal import for the pharmaceutical companies of the 20th and 21st centuries wishing to expand their markets and peddle cures for non-existent illnesses. What is particularly interesting about the history of both psychoanalysis and psychology is that they show these disciplines effectively behaving like businesses themselves, perennially advertising their wares – making a point of enlarging their sphere of influence in the absence of any real evidence to support their claims of efficacy.

The lure of categorizing was followed closely by the notion that the behavioural characteristics which underpinned these systems of classification were the result of hereditary influences. This notion found enthusiastic champions in the English upper classes – most notably Darwin's cousin, Francis Galton, who was a pioneer in that peculiarly English contribution to intellectual thought, eugenics. The goal of the eugenicists was first and foremost to rid the population of the kinds of individuals who were resident in the jails, asylums, and madhouses peppered across the country. The justification for this was that this would facilitate the maintenance at optimum levels of the biological fitness of the population. What probably underlies this specious reasoning is that the wealthy, who are always to be found lurking in the background as sponsors of eugenic movements, simply do not wish any social expenditure to be made on such 'deviant' people. Public expenditure on the poor, the sick, the disadvantaged, particularly during times of economic uncertainty, is seen as a threat to the unbounded accumulation of personal wealth to the optimum levels the rich desire.

The usual array of interventions which the eugenicists proposed (and still propose) revolves around interference with the reproductive capacities of members of the despised social groups – death being the ultimate sanction to reproductive curtailment. From the outset, the assumption was that the unfortunate characters they so objected to owed their place in the social order not to the vagaries of circumstance, nor the unlucky turns of chance in life, but to their defective biological inheritance. The Nazis used this philosophy to bolster their racial pseudoscience. It enjoyed popular support amongst the German psychologists of the day. Richards reminds us that it was the psychologists who supported the Nazi regime who "were at the forefront of the recognition of professional psychology" (1994, p.457). The twin study method, the beloved but flawed methodology used by psychologists in the investigation of genetic influences on behaviour, was created in the midst of the National Socialist era by regime-supporting scientists. Psychology has been a regular accomplice to mass crime; indeed it was a key part of the greatest mass crime in history – the Holocaust – and no doubt will be a part of the next one. This is courtesy amongst other things of its regular assists to populist criminal regimes[1] such as those of the UK and US, its usefulness to the surveillance society, and its able contributions to the reification of all forms of disobedience, whether political, social or interpersonal, as individual dysfunction.

Galton, Pearson and later Spearman – leading figures in the history of statistics and well known to generations of psychology students – sought to bolster their credo of ruling-class superiority by creating a scientific basis for it rooted in the embryonic science of statistics. Galton for example pioneered the use of correlation techniques, later used to investigate the relationship between the IQs of parents and their offspring. Galton was the son of a banker, from an extended family which contained many rich bankers. He set about trying to demonstrate that high intelligence was inborn, effectively rubber-stamping the social position of the wealthy gifted people he studied. In Galton's eyes, it was they who were the most intelligent and, duly endowed by nature, in the grand tradition of British justificatory rhetoric, were destined to rule. In his theoretical formulations, intelligence, it transpired, behaved exactly like money. There was marked inequality in the amounts which people 'possessed' and what they did have could be passed on to their offspring. While the mechanism for the transfer of money was simple legal and social expedient, the inheritance of the propensity for intelligence was some presumed biological mystery. Not surprisingly these notions were taken up with gusto by ideologues of the ruling class. Galton's ideas, like those of the social Darwinists in general, in effect legitimised inequality; these were the same ideas of biological determinism which ever since have been employed to legitimise unrestrained capitalism as the highest and inevitable expression of human nature (see Rose, Lewontin & Kamin, 1984).

Developments in statistics, built upon the contributions of Galton, Pearson and Spearman, were to prove particularly useful for psychologists when they began to address the measurement and quantification of intelligence. The issue of measurement, added to the weight attached to classification and inheritance, played a decisive role in psychology's eventual acceptance as a science and its increased social and political role.

Notwithstanding Kant's earlier objections, nobody seemed to mind all that much that the subject still lacked any firm central theoretical basis (indeed it still lacks it), had no established body of facts from which to proceed and couldn't satisfactorily define what its subject matter was. The idea that intelligence could be measured grew from Binet's early work with Parisian school children. Whilst Binet had sought simply to find a way of assisting the disadvantaged to benefit more fully from the system of education they had, the desire to measure children's capacity to reason and to give it both a label and a number was American-inspired. In the race to develop and quantify intelligence Binet's progressive idea was quickly left behind. So was born the IQ (intelligence quotient); initially the term signalled the discrepancy between a child's chronological age and the age at which they performed intellectually. This was eventually replaced by a statistical determination of IQ based on the distribution of IQ scores in a population, standardised by age.

Psychologists approached the newly fashionable IQ test with an unchallenged commitment to a hereditarian position and thus began the long and dubious tradition of inferring genetic contributions to human behavior, most notably with respect to intelligence, criminality and mental health but also to social position. IQ data based on twin studies conducted by knighted psychologist Cyril Burt was put to use in the UK by the governing elite to encourage separate streams of education for middle-class and working-class children. The 11-plus exam used to implement this survives in some parts of the UK still today. Burt's data was eventually found to have been faked. Nonetheless the hereditarian claims for intelligence and school performance continue undiminished. For example a study published toward the end of 2013 (Shakeshaft et al) which received extensive press coverage claimed that genetic influences accounted for over half the variation in GCSE exam results. This was greeted almost ecstatically by Conservative government ministers. In the study the researchers compared exam performance of identical twins with that of non-identical twins and argued that if the identical twins' exam scores were more alike than those of non-identical twins the difference was due to genetics rather than environment.

This reasoning was based on a long-standing and heavily criticised assumption made by psychologists who use the twin study method. Identical twins are largely genetically identical (i.e. they share 100 per cent of their genes) while non-identical twins share on average 50 per cent of their genes. The assumption that any differences between them must be genetic is based on (amongst other things) what is known as the equal environments assumption, that the environments of identical twins are no more similar than the environments of non-identical twins. It is widely known that this assumption is false and there is a mountain of evidence to show that it is. Despite what the authors of the study claimed, twin studies cannot disentangle the effects of genes from environment. Within the paper the authors in fact admitted that the entire credibility of the genetic interpretation of their results rests on the equal environments assumption. They wrote "limitations of the present study include general limitations of the twin method, most notably the equal environments assumption – that environmentally-caused similarity is equal for MZ and DZ twins" (p.8). Following this the authors then made the astounding claim that "the equal environments assumption has survived several tests of its validity," a claim that is demonstrably not true. Identical twins are known to a) like each other more, b) spend more time together, c) are treated as more similar by their parents, teachers and friends, d) more often dress together, e) more often study together, f) are more likely to have the same close friends and g) are more likely to attend social events together, to name but a few (see Joseph, 2004). In short not only were the study and therefore the results premised on an unsupportable assumption, but the authors supported their unsupportable claims by simply lying about the basis from which they had drawn their conclusions.

Besides the problems mentioned above there are further serious methodological problems which make any straightforward interpretation of twin study research impossible. Even if one were to examine a situation where one knew in advance that the relative contributions from genes and environment were equal this would not show up in the results. The methodology would actually produce results showing a greater genetic contribution to variability in performance. This is simply because genetic relatedness can be measured with far greater precision than can the effects of the environment. In the statistical models used in the analysis, the variable measured with greater precision (i.e. genetics) would absorb the shared variance. Space doesn't permit a full technical discussion of the problems with the methodology but there is credible and serious scientific literature on it and it is well known. The trouble is the behaviour genetics lobby routinely ignore it along with all the limitations attached to their methods.

That this paper was published in a leading scientific journal with no mention of these problems illustrates how corrupted the behaviour genetics community has become, and how their work owes more to unquestioned ideological belief than 'pure' science. The complexity of the processes involved in examining genetic material, as well as the difficulties involved in appreciating the limitations of mathematical models, has allowed them to not only make unsupportable claims but to avoid any critical public scrutiny of their methods. One factor in this is the nature of the press. Firstly most journalists do not possess the technical knowledge they require to challenge what they are told and secondly significant sections of the press are in any case attached to the same ideological agenda as the researchers. Belief in the importance of genetic influences over environmental ones is of course a regular feature of right-wing political discourse. If there is something wrong then boiling everything down to genetics means that there is no need to change the environment. Any change required must take place in the people exposed to it. This is a message that psychology routinely reinforces. Business as usual prevails – big business that is, and bad science.

What is Psychology?

By the beginning of the 20th century – with an experimental and statistical form of psychology gaining acceptance – it was obvious that there was no longer any continuity between the original use of the term 'psychology' and the present day one. Though contemporary psychology sometimes still describes itself as the science of mind and behaviour, few practitioners think that the mind has any useful reference beyond a metaphorical one or a means to lure and maintain public interest.

Psychology's early meaning at least had the virtue of possessing a single focus – a desire to understand the soul and to develop knowledge of it. The psychology which stepped into the limelight of the 20th century had none of this. At the birth of its experimental inception, the Holy Grail for practitioners was to have professional recognition and academic respectability conferred on them. The way they believed they would get this was for psychology to be given scientific status. They sought to court a wider public opinion rather than address the deeply difficult problem that they lacked any integrated theory of emotion, thought and behaviour. This was, in essence, what Freud had attempted – at the expense it turned out of wider acceptance of psychoanalysis as a science. Wundt and the other psycho-physiologists of his generation surrendered in the face of this difficulty and turned to anything that was amenable to quantification – reaction times, the number of items in a list one could remember, the duration of simple perceptual events etc. In the 21st century with a shining array of technology – from the EEG (electroencephalograph) which measures the strength of electrical signals emanating from the brain, to the MRI (Magnetic

Resonance Imaging) which indicates which regions of the brain are active – the problem is much the same: no baseline theory to connect the wealth of data these machines produce.

With no theory to capture or explain or understand what it means to be human, the subject remains tied to quantification for quantification's sake. Psychologists seem unable to agree on what their subject is or even how to study it. Because of this major rifts permeate the discipline. There is an inability to agree on what the focus should be on: what people do or say, what they think or what they feel? There are further divisions concerning what the appropriate aims of research should be – i.e. on what the discipline is trying to achieve as well the methods appropriated to try and achieve these aims. Perhaps the only thing that psychologists who call themselves scientists seem able to agree on is that their 'science' involves the measurement and/or classification of people into distinct types or categories and that appropriate procedures to test hypotheses involve the use of statistical tests.

The possibility that one might study the whole person has seldom occurred to psychologists. It has however happened at least once. Kelly's (1955) personal construct theory argued for a root and branch takeover of psychology, using both quantitative and qualitative methods, in order to redefine it as the study of persons. This is an approach with enormous potential, though now seldom mentioned in polite psychological circles. After promising much, it was quickly relegated to the fringes of 'personality' psychology and, before running aground, fell prey to recruits from psychiatry and business. These individuals, no doubt seeking spiritual solace from the *raison d'être* of their usual occupations – renowned for their respective contributions to human misery – moved in for a feeding frenzy on the decaying corpus of radical psychology. This attempt aside, we are left with a fragmented discipline, comprising a multitude of separate fields, many of which have little or nothing to do with each other. They are in effect a series of mini-psychologies: biological psychology, developmental psychology, personality and individual differences, cognitive psychology, evolutionary psychology, social psychology, health psychology, occupational psychology, educational psychology, clinical psychology and counselling psychology. Across these various domains there is no common heritage, nor even commitment to a common set of methodologies. To cover the cracks there is bolted onto every course in psychology a course or series of courses in research methods. But even here the problems multiply. Adherence to statistical methods is favoured only by those of a scientific bent. Those of a more critical persuasion are simply not convinced, point to numerous problems with positivist quantitative research methods and increasingly turn to qualitative methods which at least on occasion are employed to give expression to the voices of disadvantaged, marginalised and oppressed groups.

The continuity of psychology as a coherent and unified discipline over time is an illusion. From its inception to the present day it has leapfrogged from one stance to another. From Wundt's psychophysics (in parallel with Freud's psychoanalysis) to Watsonian and Skinnerian Behaviourism in the 1920s and 1930s to the cognitive revolution of the 1950s and 1960s it has produced a series of conflicting approaches. Although Behaviourism has been seen as self-evidently deficient as an account of human behaviour and experience by generations of psychology students (it had no interest in experience at all; for the behaviourists only what was observable was deemed worthy of scientific interest), it lumbered on for 30 years promising nothing more than total control of human behaviour – to be engineered by subtle alterations in the environmental parameters which mould behaviour through contingencies of reward and punishment. When the cognitive revolution duly arrived it owed more to the whims of military necessity and military sponsorship than scientific development. A new generation of complex weapons was deemed desirable by the military-industrial complex. These would be equipped with servo-control mechanisms capable of negotiating their way to targets, capable of perceptually analysing their surroundings and capable of decision-making independent from their controllers. At the same time sleep deprivation research was premised on the need to know how well military personnel could function under battlefield conditions where sleep might be a luxury. These concerns and not purely scientific ones prompted enormous investment in psychology. This continues still. Psychology's long cooperation with war aims and military tasks is examined in Chapter 4. The defence industries, it should not be forgotten, are the military wing of industrial capitalism. Psychology eschewed the soul a long time ago; if the soul still existed within the discipline, it would no doubt be sold to the highest bidder. In the next chapter we examine psychology's relationship to the ideological bedrock of capitalism a little more closely.

Chapter 2

Psychology and Ideology

Psychology by no means holds the 'secret' of human affairs, simply because this 'secret' is not of a psychological order.
(Politzer, cited in Sève, 1978, p.9)

Psychology as Science: Individualism and Ideology

When asked to consider what the study of psychology comprises, many lay people will probably think of Freud or Jung or imagine it is about reading people's minds or learning to develop or possess esoteric insights into human behaviour. Others may well have assimilated popular science presentations which suggest all we need to know or could ever know about the human condition is to be found in the brain. So, on the one hand we have the popular representations of psychoanalysts delving into the secrets of the mind by way of learned and compassionate therapy, and on the other we have the powerful message that the mind is the brain – whose mysteries science can uncover, just as it can the mysteries of any other physical object in the universe. These divergent points of view – between psychology as art and psychology as natural science – have bedevilled the discipline since its inception and, never having been satisfactorily reconciled, have led to bitter conflicts within it.

In many ways the contrasting images of psychology available to the general public, which we may characterise somewhat simply as the couch and the brain scanner, have presented a very misleading picture of the things that psychologists do and why they do them. These two strands of representation not surprisingly enter the fray from very different quarters and have quite different sources and kinds of support. The arguments put forward concern questions not simply about what kinds of knowledge we wish to have about human beings, and what we want to do with that knowledge, but also how these different forms of knowledge relate to existing systems of power in the world at large. As we will see later in this book, how psychological knowledge and perspectives have been employed in the world by the powerful have important implications for the kind of future we will live in and the kind of world that is possible. At present much of this knowledge and discussion has been the sole preserve of elite groups – academics, scientists, politicians, military planners and business leaders. It is imperative not only that the limitations of this knowledge are widely understood, but that the public also exert a much greater influence than they have until now on the kinds of psychological questions which are asked and which are truly of relevance and interest to them.

The very possibility that psychological knowledge itself may not be politically neutral is one which many psychologists do not wish to face. It is also a question which has been kept firmly away from the public gaze and from the majority of students who undertake a degree in the subject. This chapter will examine these conflicting types of psychology and attempt to make clear how they relate to major systems of political thought, in particular the set of ideas and beliefs which form the ideological lynchpin of the capitalist system. Psychology as natural science is not only the dominant form in which it is practiced; it is also the preferred form from the point of view of the existing social and political structure. There are a number of reasons for this, linked to the assumptions which are embedded in the theories and practices of experimental psychology.

First of all this approach holds that the individual is the primary reality from which we understand the world. Echoing Margaret Thatcher's infamous maxim that there is no such thing as society, the framework implies that society is simply a collection of individuals and that the use of the term 'social' refers to nothing more than the environment of the individual. By

an amazing coincidence it is also a cornerstone of the philoso-
phies of 'rational' self-interest and individualism upon which the
entire field of economics is predicated. Inevitably this
encourages a reductionist analysis of all social phenomena. From
urban rioting, political protest and changing social mores, to
widespread inequality, drug use and ill-health, it all comes down
to what is going on inside the individual. It is also how the
catastrophes of finance capital are explained to us. It is not the
entire system of classical economics or finance capitalism, built
on greed and exploitation, which is at fault – merely the actions
of rogue, possibly defective individuals. The proposed solutions
to deal with this are consequently minor reformist tinkering to
enable better detection of the aberrant miscreants, individuals
who we soon invariably learn were operating under 'stress' or
dealing with a 'drug problem.'

One additional assumption needs to be incorporated into this
setup in order to make it appear plausible. The scientific
approach is intent on discovering universal laws of nature –
principles which govern the operation of matter (i.e. the world of
things) and which operate in the same way in all times and
places. Consequently psychology must assume it is discovering
and elucidating principles which apply to all cultures, in all
places, at all times in human history. It has the gumption to
continue with such claims despite a number of quite obvious
problems, not least of which is the fact that a majority of the
work published to date has come from research conducted with
North American volunteer students. Not only are North
Americans not typical of the world's population, but neither are
volunteers and neither are students, who for example are known
for being friendlier, brighter, younger and less conventional than
the general population. And then of course there are the
problems which arise from the methods which are used to gather
information. Experimental methods assume what is called
ecological validity, which means that there are no serious

problems in extrapolating results from laboratory-based studies to the bigger, messier, more complicated real world.

One upshot then of all these assumptions is that basic concepts which have been developed within psychology such as 'the self,' 'personality,' 'attitudes,' 'intelligence' or 'mental illness' are the properties of individuals, are somehow a-historic, and exist independent of culture as real entities in the world. In fact with a bit of reflection once can see that there are no reasons why we such accept such claims at all. The difficulty one faces when trying to argue this is that psychologists have already been so successful in disseminating these constructs throughout the social spaces we inhabit that we almost have to believe that they are true. However social space is similarly inhabited by concepts such as zombies, vampires, ghosts, time-travellers and extra-terrestrials, not to mention The Labour Party as an organisation that stands up for the interests of working people; so one can quickly see that a word does not necessarily carry the world with it. The map, we have been warned often enough, is not the territory – in the case of psychological propensities not even a finger pointing to the moon. History is of course of great importance when considering the psychological nature of the ideas that we take to represent reality. A couple of hundred years ago one would have been hard-placed to find anyone who did not believe that they possessed an immortal soul. Nowadays this is much less common, though few would now doubt that we all 'have' a 'personality.'

The psychologisation of our life in the world which thus proceeds has a number of extremely subtle aspects to it. Features of the wider world, and here in particular I am referring to aspects of the socio-economic organisation of the world under capitalism, come to be understood as psychological properties residing in the bodies and brains of individuals.

The nearest psychology gets to addressing the structural violence and inequality built into the capitalist system is through social dominance theory which reduces systemic properties to individual ones. Thus the system is explained in terms of the psychological orientation of individuals toward dominance together with the degree to which they desire group relations which are unequal. In true psychological fashion this is considered as a measurable personality variable – 'social dominance orientation' – and the historical, structural and cultural changes in class relationships, from slavery through feudalism to capitalism, are accordingly largely ignored.

The logic of the capitalist mode of production in effect has been interiorised as perennial psychological attributes. Intelligence and personality for example are used to distinguish the performance and productivity of workers, while the incessant demands made of workers, which they must meet in order to keep their job, earn a wage and thus survive, are interiorised as a list of psychological traits: 'agreeableness,' 'conscientiousness,' 'punctuality,' 'vitality,' 'hardiness' or 'resilience' for example. If one fails to conform to the demands of industrial logic then the new discipline of positive psychology comes in to explain that the reason for this lies not in the demands made or the context in which they are made but in the hapless and culpable individual who, perforce, must have a 'problem' and hasn't developed the required coping skills and psychological characteristics needed to deal with a collapsing industrial society and widespread ecological devastation. Beyond their deficient coping skills they may also have an 'attitude' problem – with the attitude considered as some hard-wired neuro-cognitive structure residing in the brain rather than a response to circumstances – or if the recalcitrance is of a more serious nature altogether such that the person refuses to work entirely or wilts under the punishing schedule of it, then they can be deemed to have a mental health problem (see Chapter 3). More direct challenges still to the established system of deference and privilege may be passed off as 'anti-social personality' or downright 'criminality.' In effect psychology contributes to the privatising of responsibility in a world where transnational corporations behave with no responsibility. In the midst of the mess which envelops us, good adjustment is mapped out by psychologists as happiness not protest.

One of the more recent psychological 'conditions' which arouses the concern of employers is 'autism.' It has been argued that the massive increases in the diagnosis of this condition (note – there are no biological tests to identify it) coincide with the need for what is called 'emotional labour' in the workforce. It is no longer enough just to shift product – one must now do it with a smile, with 'sincerity,' with a friendly touch. From cabin crew keeping irritated passengers at bay on long-haul flights, through lecturers 'enhancing the student experience' in higher education, to sex-workers faking the appearance of love for their clients, emotional labour is in vogue. Consider the almost-real girlfriend experience – now *de rigueur* in the escort business (Sanders, 2008) – to be compared for favourability with the all-too-real bank-manager experience which is now *de rigueur* in the course of an education in psychology. Fake sincerity is in and it is everywhere, and it is no longer enough just to fake it. It must be real even as one is faking it.

The manipulation of psychological states, feelings and senti-ments thus plays a key role in market transactions in the 21st century. Con artists employing fraud and deceit have always made use of them. What we now have is merely an extension of this strategy. People have to be cheated out of their money. With scripted emotion it is less likely the customer will complain. Faking of emotions now demonstrates 'good' psychological skills – like numeracy and literacy – much needed by employers. It is not hard therefore to see why psychology is now big business and why it is a major contributor to the escalating unreality of reality. As life comes to feel more unreal we are sold virtual realities to enhance it, which of course only serves to make it yet more unreal. These versions of simulated reality unsurprisingly sell us (actually more often than not such false worlds are sold to males) copious amounts of violence – supposedly to represent some dystopian near-future when it will be every man for himself and military experience will be a prized asset even for a perfunctory visit to the local supermarket. Food now being a scarce commodity, one will have to machine gun one's way through the bread queues in the hell-hole future world. Psychology, it may appear surprising, has never taken much interest in either emotional labour or denial; to read anything instructive on these one must turn to sociology. Perhaps the fear is that contemplation of these processes will alert the prospective student to the dangerous possibilities of waking up, insight and rebellion. Psychologists have shown no theoretical interest in the manipulation (overt or covert) of people's behaviour by outside agencies. They have been content merely to supply and perfect the technology for others to do it.

As a final means of avoiding the moral dilemmas inherent in asking why the world is as it is, psychology has turned to evolutionary theory. The result, 'evolutionary psychology,' described by Hilary Rose as "a moral and intellectual cop-out" (2001, p.126), has, like the last two Gulf Wars, been largely an Anglo-American championed phenomenon. The reasons for this are not hard to fathom. The idea is to explain away contemporary features of the social world – a world subject to the US-led global neo-liberal economic orthodoxy – as biological adaptations rooted in our evolutionary past. The view that gets promoted is that human nature has been essentially fixed for the past 100-600,000 years and that certain aspects of contemporary life – class privilege and male violence against women to name but two – are biologically set. With biology endorsed as destiny, arguments from evolutionary psychology have been used to argue against welfare provision, a position also favoured by some psychologists who champion the so-called bio-psycho-social model of health. Welfare provision for the rich in the form of bank bailouts, tax cuts and unchallenged tax-avoidance have curiously never set the psychological pulses running and remain untheorised by the legions of psychologists who would be happy to see the entire social world explained in psychological terms. In evolutionary psychology we thus see echoes of the kind of ruthless social-Darwinist mind-set which so animated Germany's National Socialists in the 1930s in their defence against the collective 'evils' of communism and egalitarianism.

Psychology then in its theoretical development has been concerned to create ideologically appropriate 'interior' products for consumption in the capitalist world. As psychologisation proceeds at breakneck pace, we consume these in ever greater amounts and when things go wrong in our lives we look for what is wrong with us. As we saw in the last chapter the development of modern psychology has gone hand in hand with the development of the security/surveillance state. With the dissemination and internalisation of psychological language goes the phenomenon of self-blame and self-scrutiny. The answers to life's problems paradoxically may be more likely to appear if we dispense with rather than consult ever more the armies of psychological experts ready to advise and assist us in endless self-surveillance. The message is clear: it is not alright to be different. The psychological language used to explain the world however has other adverse effects. This is because it has also been shaped by the commoditisation of private experience.

Rather than seeing ourselves as organic living beings changing in flux with the ongoing world we come to view ourselves as a collection of components which we 'have' or indeed which we 'lack.' What we lack we can buy, replace or upgrade – maybe by popping in a pill or by interfacing with micro-technology to transform ourselves into cyborgs. We have thereby come to own our 'selves.' As the likes of Madonna, David Bowie and Lady Gaga repeatedly demonstrate, these ephemeral selves have no substance and like any other product can be discarded when the time is right or when the price is right. No wonder many people feel empty. All this has not been an overnight phenomenon. In its heyday the menace of lobotomy was described by its advocates as a 'personality rejuvenator' and the recipients of this barbaric procedure (it is still practiced) did indeed get a 'new' personality, but at the cost of a soul.

As well as theorising hypothetical 'internal' processes[2] which underlie personhood, the job of the psychologist has also been to promote their discipline or branch of it, so that the population are duped into finding what they say credible. This is done in much the same manner as one promotes a brand of washing powder or chocolates. In the course of my own career in psychology I have been advised many times to promote 'social' psychology, 'health' psychology or 'psychology' itself. I have even of course been asked to promote myself in order to make myself more 'marketable.' In this way psychologists become hired hands for capitalism. Few other disciplines carry on like this. While working in Epidemiology and Public Health (the branch of medicine dealing with population health) for several years I was never asked to promote anything. However one does note the increasing promotion of 'science' in the media along with the notion of promoting science in schools and in public spaces such as the Science Museum. This can be understood as a feature of 'Big Science' in which scientific activity increasingly revolves around large-scale projects funded by government, groups of governments or corporations and scientific progress becomes synonymous with the advance of corporate and capitalist aspirations. Science has been under a corporate siege for some time now and if the cavalry ever come to relieve it, one can be sure there will be no psychologists riding to the rescue.

Before we begin to consider a different form of psychology, one which already exists in embryonic form, we need to get an appreciation of the scale on which academic psychology functions as a vector for carrying the 'meme' and ethos of individualism into the wider population. A British Psychological Society (BPS) report in 2013 documented that psychology was now the fourth most popular A-level choice for students in the UK, the subject having undergone an exponential rise over the past 20 years. In 2010 there were 55,000 entries for the full A-level and 100,000 entries for the AS-level. The report also states that by the same year the number of undergraduate students had reached 77,000, a figure which has more than doubled in just over 10 years. It goes on to say:

> One consequence of the growth in psychology courses at all levels is the increasing proportion of the population of the UK who have taken a programme of study in the subject. This is growing at over 100,000 people every year and has been near to this level for a generation. In 2012 in the UK there were about 750,000 17-year-olds, meaning that over 13 per cent of them had taken an AS qualification in the subject; if you added in the number taking psychology as part of their courses in health and social care, for example, then a picture develops of a population with a growing awareness of the basic ideas of psychology (p.8).

While the denizens of the BPS consider this growth in psychological literacy to be a good thing, there are actually considerable grounds for being alarmed. No research to date has been conducted on the effects of this potentially massive influence. One can however predict what some of these might be: increased labelling of people who are considered different, increased propensity to medicalise behaviour, increased propensity to psychologise what are ethical, social and political problems in the world and with it to blame individuals for the ills which have befallen them. Given the dominance of the positivistic approach, this also suggests the growth in psychological awareness will carry with it an increased tendency to de-historicise human actors and to project onto the past the beliefs of today. All of these possibilities decrease rather than increase the chances of us producing viable and long-lasting solutions to the pressing problems humanity faces.

Psychology as Life History: Existence and Politics

The first rumblings of disquiet in psychology began to surface in the 1960s and early 1970s. Critics began to question not only the routine use of deception in social psychological experiments but also the validity of laboratory methods for understanding the complex social worlds we inhabit. Added to these issues were concerns about just how widely findings were able to travel from their North-American home and still speak to people in other cultures. Western researchers increasingly see their culture imposed on others throughout the rest of the world. Enchanted by their unconscious imperialistic stance, they mistakenly conclude from this that there is a de facto global human culture to which their research speaks and that the principles they construct from their work are therefore universal. The crisis, as it came to be called, rumbled on a few years, with the most critical voices coming from Europe, where workers could draw from a greater range of intellectual traditions than the pragmatic approach most favoured in the US. Thus European social psychology offered insights from Marxism, psychoanalysis, feminism, post-modernism and the emerging paradigms of social constructionism and social representations.

A key piece of work to emerge in this period however did come from the US. In a key article Kenneth Gergen (1992) rejected the experimental approach out of hand and its claims to universality, denouncing it as "individualistic and exploitative" (p.17). All psychological findings, he argued, were effectively "socially and historical embedded," rooted in specific times and places and limited to the culture in which they were generated.

What could be true today might change tomorrow. As such the social world was not a given 'out there' to be investigated by the impartial natural scientist, but something in a continual process of construction by human actors, including researchers themselves. How one relates to this world then contributes to the state of the world which comes next. Science has worked well, it is argued, because it is a method geared toward understanding the behaviour of inanimate objects. Whenever science studies living creatures and systems as inanimate objects there are problems. Unlike inanimate objects the behaviour of people in objective three-dimensional space is a function of their experience of themselves, their experience of others and their experience of the world around them, as well as the behaviour of other persons, institutions and material objects. Thus a new vision for psychology must perforce embrace human subjectivity.

The emphasis on subjectivity has breathed new life into psychoanalysis. Though dismissed by the scientific brethren, psychoanalysis has long been associated with radical critiques of the social order. Seeking to explain why, in the midst of economic crisis, the masses had turned to the Nazis rather than the Communists, Reich's (1946) *Mass Psychology of Fascism* attributed the fascist character structure to a systematic repression of sexuality which gave rise to unhappy, neurotic people and was responsible for aggression and sadism and a desire for power over others. For Reich however this was not purely a psychological matter; the origins of the fascist's character structure, he considered, lay in the "social institutions that hatch him daily" (p.18). Reich to a degree sought to practice what he preached, actively campaigning for free distribution of contraceptives, abolition of laws against abortion and legal distinctions between the married and unmarried, improved sex education and treatment rather than punishment for sex offenses. In 1930s Germany, neither the fledgling psychoanalytic establishment nor the Communist Party was ready for this. He was expelled from both. It is to Reich that we owe the term 'sexual politics.' His influence in contemporary psychotherapy and culture has been immense, but he remains absent from the curricula of every psychology degree.

Eric Fromm, whose influence on mainstream psychology is also sadly negligible, has probably been foremost among the psychoanalytic fraternity to make use of Marx's insights. Fromm argued that in both Marx's early works (*The Economic and Philosophical Manuscripts*) and later works (*Capital*) there was a treasure trove of hopes and insights for students of the human character. He considered Marx a humanist, who saw the human character as pregnant with possibilities. Unlike the fixed, deterministic view of human nature that traditional psychology supplies, Marx's view was that the human 'essence' unfolded historically; that our true nature could only be realised through our active participation in and development of the social and economic order; that we could only be known by what we do. The spirit of Marx's position is expressed by Christian Bale's *Batman* during the course of the first film of the franchise (Nolan, 2005). "It's not who I am underneath," Bale's character intones, "but what I do that defines me." Marx envisioned this historical process as leading to the creation of a free unalienated type of person. These ideas foreshadow both the later existentialists[3] and social constructionists who argue that the human condition is at once an inalienable mystery and is constructed in collaboration with others in a world not of our choosing. From where and when we are cast into the world we make our own history, blighted by the possibilities of alienation and false consciousness, but our consciousness is always specifically rooted in our day to day material, social, historical circumstances. Fromm stresses Marx's preoccupation with life-affirming human activity as opposed to the deadening hand of capital which creates false wants and needs and makes of everything – material objects, relationships, experiences and people –

a commodity. For Fromm (1977), as for Marx, capitalism puts before us a choice between two different modes of life: "To Have or To Be." Fromm's discussion of love is a reminder of the great and noble possibilities latent in human life and its antithesis to the marketised love of capitalist dreams.

R. D. Laing and Slavoj Žižek have followed Reich and Fromm in bringing the tools of psychoanalysis to bear on problems in the social and political order. Laing attempted a fusion of existentialism and Marxism in examining the role of the family in the meaning of psychological disturbance, while Žižek has likened our responses to the death throes of capitalism in the 21st century to a mass grief reaction. Both denial and repression figure strongly in these explanatory notions of our acceptance of and refusal to challenge the existing order. Psychoanalysis however has not been without its critics on the left. Though Parker views it as "the 'repressed other' of positivistic experimental psychology," (2007, p.120) he sees in it the same danger which inhabits academic psychology: the tendency to reduce what are the products of the capitalist economic phenomena (e.g. alienation, commodification and reification) to the inner world of the individual's mind (see Chapter 3).

This different strand of psychology cultivated by these critics – by drawing on emancipatory discourses such as Marxism and feminism – has suggested a different way of doing psychology: with different rules, different methods, different values, different kinds of data, and a different kind of knowledge generated. With the researcher actively considered as a part of the social field under investigation, all knowledge is relational. This suggests a different role for academics – one in which neutrality has been banished and in its place there is a bias for truth and a firm stance against oppression. These attacks on the scientific status of social psychology inevitably produced a backlash. The hopes that critical psychologists initially entertained for a paradigm change in the discipline were eventually washed away. Those in the positivist camp simply refused to engage with the arguments mustered by their critics. The crisis eventually faded from view, albeit with none of the issues settled; it remains a seething low-level conflict. It would be a mistake however to consider the dispute a stalemate. Positivist psychology with an experimental individualistic outlook remains highly dominant and the reason for this has to do with one of the major ideas which critical theorists threw into the ring: this is the question of power.

Foucault's work on the history of sexuality and madness embraced the genealogical methods of the German philosopher Friedrich Nietzsche; this essentially involved tracing the historical origins of ideas. Whereas Nietzsche had sought to situate human morality in historical circumstances and therefore as something not God-given, Foucault turned to the histories of madness and sexuality. His work helped establish the view that how humans experience themselves in the world – our subjec-tivity as it were – is always historically situated and constructed. Secondly Foucault's work played a seminal role in drawing attention to how relations of power between different groups shape this subjectivity, and how the processes which sustain power relations operate in part through the linguistic repertoires of the day. This in turn has led to a huge interest in language and discourse, so that rather than language being seen (as in natural science) as an unproblematic transparent mediator of truth, it is language that is a vehicle for sustaining or indeed challenging power. In this way the issues of language and power have come to be seen as inseparable. Language shapes the reality we see, is a tool in how the nature of world is revealed to us and in a manner of speaking reveals the entities in the world we are led to believe in.

Critical psychologists have taken these insights of Foucault and applied them to their own discipline. They have asked: under what historical circumstances does psychology as a bona fide discipline appear and how does its emergence and development relate to existing and changing systems of power? How does the knowledge it generates challenge, sustain or promote power and where? This means that the eternal reality of psychological phenomenon must be called into question. We are now in a better position to understand how the contention arises that psychology theorises interiorised states as reflections of the capitalist logic of production. Psychology does this through its subservient position to existing systems of power. Perennially unsure of its status, from its inception to the present day it has sought to find its place within existing systems of power relations. The multiplication of interiorised states has led to the present situation where the entire population have placed themselves under constant self-surveillance. Too fat, too thin, too happy, too sad, too angry, too anxious, too quiet, too sexual, not sexual enough; the list is endless. The gaze from the powerful other – the forces of the state – is increasingly being replaced by the internal gaze of the historically situated subject.

It is no accident that psychology emerged around the same time as the feudal order made way for the capitalist order. Both Kvale (2003) and Fromm (1942) have discussed how the institutions and practices of the church (including confession), both during and prior to the Reformation, to say nothing of the insecurity of the changing historical landscape, contributed to the birth of psychology. Church doctrine, together with confession, merged with the nascent individualizing language of merchant capital to produce the "interiorization of the soul and the privatization of the self" (Kvale, 2003, pp.581-3) along with a mechanised view of the world. The status of psychology is, and has thus always been, primarily ideological.

Chapter 3

Capitalism and Mental Health

*Modern academic and experimental psychology is to a large extent
a science dealing with alienated man, studied by alienated investi-
gators with alienated and alienating methods.*
(Fromm, 1973, p.69)

*The privatisation of stress has been part of a project that has aimed
at an almost total destruction of the concept of the public – the very
thing upon which psychic well-being fundamentally depends.*
(Fisher, 2011)

Alienation

If we are to satisfactorily consider the set of relationships which
exist between the capitalist system of production, distribution
and exchange and our subjective well-being we have to consider
not only how this system impacts upon our well-being, but also
the very conceptual categories which we employ to understand
our subjective states. It is the latter set of categories, bequeathed
to us from psychiatry and psychology, which is largely responsible not only for our considerable confusion about how we are
affected by living within the capitalist system, but also for our
ongoing confusion about what is commonly called mental
health. Before we consider how the dominant medico-psycho-
logical framework for understanding mental health – as now
enshrined in the *Diagnostic and Statistical Manual for Mental
Disorders* (the DSM, currently in its fifth edition) – serves to
support and reinforce the capitalist system, we must first
examine a perspective on our actual and potential well-being
which is uncontaminated by the mores of the current mental
health system and which casts considerable light on the

problems contained within it. This perspective is alienation.

'Alienation' is a term poorly understood but frequently bandied about – although not in psychology one must say. Marx first proposed using it in his *Economic and Philosophical Manuscripts* (see Fromm, 2011) to answer what was for him one of the central questions – if not *the* central question – we face when trying to understand the human condition: why do we participate in our own oppression? Marx saw alienation as a form of estrangement from our inherent human nature, a dislocation from the inherent life-affirming possibilities of existence. For him this was inevitable for anyone living in a socially stratified society where the means of production lay in the hands of one class – the capitalists – to the detriment of the overwhelming majority of the population who were workers (actual or potential). In Marx's view both capitalist and worker were alienated from their fundamental humanity with the form of this alienation coming simultaneously in several distinct varieties, all of which have considerable bearing on how psychology as a discipline perpetuates alienation and serves the ethos of capital.

Arguably the most fundamental form of this alienation is the alienation from oneself whereby one loses the right to consider oneself the author/director of one's own actions. This is not difficult to imagine as one behaviourally fulfils the wishes of one's bosses from the vantage point of one's allotted place on the assembly line, or reads from the company script in the hot-house of a telephone centre, dutifully obeying the commands from on-high to sell anything from windows to life insurance to legions of unwilling customers. In advanced capitalist societies such alienation has now filtered through to so-called intellectual professions: computer programmers, for example, writing code which will form part of the operating system of machines designed to kill or maim; or academics forced to write endless business-friendly grant applications to secure a living from the corporate table. This alienation from ourselves goes hand in hand with alienation from work and the economic alienation that ensues from it. Our capacity to act fully autonomously in accordance with our basic creative, loving nature is transformed under the conditions of the omnipresent market into programmed activity. This not only eats into the possibility of engaging with work in a way which is psychologically satisfying, but separates us from any say in how the products of our labour are to be used.

Herein, though, lays a problem – one central to the operation of the mental health system. Under current rules one is not supposed to realise that one is alienated; that one performs actions authored elsewhere. If, in a moment of awareness, a person claims that they are a puppet merely responding mechanically and obediently to 'alien' orders – that their body is in fact an empty shell controlled by external alien powers – they are likely to find themselves summoned to the nearest psychiatric authority, declared out of touch with reality and diagnosed with paranoid schizophrenia. If the reality of the relationship which one's own actions have to the wider forces of power breaks through into consciousness and produces signs of observable distress, the chances of psychiatric incarceration are elevated still further. The possibility that such claims – statements expressing one's predicament – might actually be accurate descriptions, albeit laced with a dash of metaphor, of one's present relationship to the wider world and the dominant system of production is simply not up for consideration. It is over 70 years since the psychoanalyst Eric Fromm commented that we believe ourselves "to be motivated by self-interest and yet" our lives are "devoted to aims which are not [our] own" (1942, p.101). These sentiments retain their capacity to disturb but they remain undiscussed within the psychological mainstream and rarely considered even on the periphery. A very effective trap for maintaining the illusion that the present system has in some way been ordained by nature and is beyond question, thus goes unchallenged.

Our alienation from ourselves and work is compounded by the forward march of technology. As Marx noted, industrial production is organised to suit the work of machines and within such a system the human worker becomes ancillary to the machine: a cog in the clockwork manufacture of commodities for use and want, but not need. From this it is a logical development that we ourselves come increasingly to resemble machines. Not only are we theorised and objectified under contemporary systems of scientific representation (which are themselves subject to capitalist domination) to be nothing other than biological and biochemical machines, but there is worse. As our daily activities, characteristics, propensities, foibles, creative works and thoughts – our very private lives in fact – are sold on the open market as entertainment, we become de facto commodities. Witness the rise of the Jerry Springer genre of daytime TV, a sub-set of reality TV in general, added to which there is *The X Factor*, the expanding global multimedia sex industry, internet dating and social media to say nothing of the vast swathes of the population reduced to mere flesh and blood extensions of their smart phones. As 'they' become smarter we become dumber: an appendage to the machine.

Alienation and dislocation from oneself necessarily implies alienation and dislocation from others. As our relationship with ourselves becomes objectified and externalised as commercial property so too do we lose the ability to define our relationships with other people. Capitalist social relations, as Eric Fromm so eloquently described, sees other people turned into things. Their intrinsic value as human beings is transformed into a value based upon how they can be used. Everybody comes to have a price and a use. They appear only as objects to be 'consumed' that they may satisfy us. Modern psychology in service to super-capitalist transnational ideology has contributed enormously to this alienated view of ourselves. As embodied, thinking, feeling, loving, experiencing creatures imbued with a sense of self, human beings have all but disappeared from the theoretical and practical mainstream of the discipline – a shock to which every generation of psychology students must rapidly adjust. Eliminated from the subject matter of the behavioural sciences, the person as a centre of experience has been supplanted by the 'zombie,' celebrated by philosopher Dan Dennett as "behaviourally indistinguishable" from a "normal human being" (1992, p.405). This helps psychologists both to evade the perennial mystery of consciousness – said to be "materialism's biggest problem" (Sheldrake, 2012, p.109) – and to continue the relentless celebration of the automatic. As we consume one another for the edification of the market, zombies and their vampire cousins raise their un-dead heads with disconcerting regularity, anywhere from late-night TV to the local high street, in what seems to be a suitable metaphor for how we are encouraged to relate to one another. This apocalyptic vision reduces human existence to a serial collectivity[4], ruthlessly competing in an eternal Darwinian struggle for survival: an essentially disorganised anti-social ensemble driven to consume, devouring all comers in its wake – much like the agents behind the international financial system exposed by Bakan (2005) as corporate psychopaths. We in the West are now literally, as well as figuratively, what we eat. We have become the alienated form of the corporate entity.

Psychology and Alienation

The forms of alienation referred to above (from self, other, work and economic control) which shape the contours of our psychological reality are compounded by the discipline of psychology which purports to be a neutral science of mind and behaviour. Rather than contesting these forms of alienation, psychology not only exacerbates them but moves to celebrate them in a positivist "carnival of inauthenticity" (Boym, 2010, p.104). It is not difficult to see how. Alienation from self is actively encouraged by psycho-biological frameworks – particularly behaviour genetics – which permeate the discipline and challenge and undermine notions of free will and responsibility. Subject to the petrifying gaze of the natural sciences, a club to which psychology yearns to belong, human beings are studied as if we were nothing more than complex mechanisms: a value-free approach to humanity which mirrors the value-free operations of the market.

This obsession with being a natural science leads to an obsession with measurement and a rigid stance which holds that the study of anything which cannot be measured – and human subjectivity and experience of the world are prime examples of what cannot be measured – is not scientific and therefore is of less importance. In the UK, the state-sponsored systems of regulation of academic workers, the Research Assessment Exercise (RAE) and Research Excellence Framework (REF), actively support this distinction. Work using anything other than quantitative methods and which enquires into forms of human subjectivity is automatically rated as being of a lower quality by academic assessors so thoroughly conditioned into market requirements that they frequently assess the supposed quality of such work without even reading it. This says everything one needs to know about the validity of the exercise. That academics themselves have mustered almost no opposition to it also says a lot about the docile and subservient pose they routinely adopt towards those in power. Work which sees human beings construed as machines – at the mercy of genetic, physiological, biochemical and computational forces – is of a kind which excites corporate decision-makers who see investment in such work as potentially profitable. The massively expanded field of face recognition stands as a shining example of this – it is the most heavily funded area of psychology and year in year out contributes to the growth of the security state.

The socially, culturally, politically, economically and histori-cally de-contextualised human being who emerges from the

centre of reductionist psychological theorising has serious consequences for how we think about the social and psychological ills
which befall us. Left utterly alone it is the individual man or
woman who must be held solely accountable for their own fate.
No external agents can be held responsible as they have already
been factored out of the scientific equation. Psychological theory
thus facilitates first of all victim-blaming: each individual
becomes the source of their mental and physical problems, a
desirable state of affairs for governments of a neo-liberal political
persuasion and for the slave master corporations to whom they
bow down. Secondly, isolated thus theoretically from the wider
human social field in which our lives unfold, our alienation from
others is magnified to the extent that even the blows inflicted on
us by others are seldom recognised. Fifty years have passed since
Laing and Esterson's (1964) ground-breaking studies of family
life. These suggested, to the chagrin of the medical profession,
that there was perhaps no such thing as schizophrenia, that even
severe psychological disturbance could be understood once
something of a person's social (and historical) situation was
comprehended. Yet despite a mountain of evidence to support
this position it continues to receive no mention in the majority of
academic psychology textbooks – books which purport to
educate us in 'abnormal' psychology. Not only is the family (a
key institution in capitalist life) protected from scrutiny in this
way by psychological and psychiatric theory but, by extension,
all other contemporary social institutions are protected along
with it; and there is no longer one in existence which has not
been infected by capitalist logic. One of the leading candidates
for driving people up the wall and out of their minds must be the
workplace. With bullying and intimidation now normative
behaviour in many UK workplaces, the slings and arrows of
outrageous managerialism have been felt by far too many.

The alienation promoted by theory has manifested itself in
other ways too. One has been the isolation of the discipline from

other social sciences, chiefly history and sociology. The result of this is that the discipline increasingly exists within an intellectual bubble and is becoming impervious to the knowledge generated outside of its rigid boundaries. A similar estrangement also exists between economics and ecology. To add to these intra-disciplinary ills, the imposition of market forces upon global higher education has had a catastrophic effect on critical thought in the discipline. The one truly social and critical branch of psychology – critical social psychology – saw not a single one of its adherents throughout the UK admitted to the last RAE under the heading of psychology. Such critical work has instead found itself a home with sociology/social policy and linguistics. But this separation can only further the development of what many now see as a bunker mentality in psychology. It is scientism or nothing. The antipathy which now exists between social and cognitive psychologists and which is routinely found in academic departments also accentuates the problem. Both camps see themselves as residing in different intellectual not to say ideological worlds. The instrumentalist view promoted within cognitive psychology – which summarily holds us to be sophisticated biological computers – also entails that other human beings, students as well as colleagues, come to be seen in terms of their 'use value,' with many a psychological career erected over the bodies of those who have been trampled on.

Last but not least, the alienation from self and others which impacts on psychologists by virtue of the content of the work they do is itself performed within a wider alienating context. There is on the one hand economic alienation arising from the corporate sponsorship and ownership of academic publishing. Most academic journals are owned by major corporations, with the authors whose work provides the copy going unpaid for their efforts. Added to this, with the ranking of journals now taking on the appearance of a sports league, perceived competition is rife. Consequently, the mantra of publish or perish – and this now means publishing in increasingly 'exclusive journals' which is a reaffirmation of the class basis of social reality – has transformed the once relatively level playing field of academic debate into one where deep status-fuelled divisions exist. The pressures to stay at the top which result from this have, in their turn, led to steep rises in both plagiarism and fraud. Squeezed on one side by these corporate pressures, the hapless psychology academic is now also squeezed from the other side by the stifling bureaucratization of higher education – with endless form filling, targets, curriculum changes and higher education newspeak occupying a large proportion of the working week.

Mystification

The case outlined so far then is that psychology as an academic discipline produces an alienating picture of the human condition. It does this by alienated workers working in an alienated economic and occupational milieu. But do the problems end there? Alas they do not. Before we proceed to examine the theoretical basis of the mental health system and its deep relation to the forces and logic of capitalism we must first consider the second component in Marx's explanation for the human propensity to surrender to subjugation. To alienation Marx added the notion of mystification. Mystification occurs most often in situations of actual or potential conflict where what is actually being done or what is taking place or being experienced is obscured behind a set of constructions which suggest something else entirely. What we see and experience happening to us is not what we are told is happening. This is a regular feature of political communication.

As an example consider the current state of the UK economy still reeling from the banking crisis of 2007/8. In the midst of this we are told that the country can no longer afford the provision of welfare to disabled people. We are fed endless stories of how the country's finances are being stretched to breaking point by feckless claimants, lazy working-class people and immigrants. The actual reality is that a massive transfer of wealth from poor to rich is taking place. Billions of pounds, far in excess of anything lost through inappropriate welfare claims, are being lost through tax avoidance by the rich. Understandably welfare recipients are confused by the sudden deluge of attacks upon them. The considerable numbers of the population who are turning against their fellow citizens in attack have been steered into avoiding seeing the true conflict. Their anger and outrage are the result of mystification. The real nature of the conflict people face – an onslaught upon their living standards by the super-rich, which is part of what Jeffrey Winters (2011) has referred to as the politics of wealth defence – is thereby evaded.

With this in mind, we can see that a good deal of psychological theory as well as being alienating is also mystifying. Conflicts between people and the everyday difficulties and stresses that people encounter (most of the psychological difficulties which people present with are actually concerned with their relationships with other people), which may sap their energy, will, joy and desire, are theoretically reconfigured as not the result of ongoing or prior difficult circumstances but defects in biochemistry or genetics which reside in themselves. In this way the reality of our problems in living become mystified as disease processes. Political, social and interpersonal issues are discussed as if they were actually medical problems – part of what psychiatrist Thomas Szasz (2007a) referred to as the medicalisation of everyday life. Marx's explanation for false consciousness (see Fromm, 2011) – identification with one's oppressors and the goals they espouse (including support for the diversionary tactics of racism, attacks on the poor etc); the defence of the status quo; refusal to recognise the fundamental nature of class conflict – is that it is produced by a combination of alienation and mystification. The irony is that a good many of the people who embark on a psychological education do so with the intention of improving people's lives. Their hopes are to effect widespread change in people's well-being. They are misled – mystified even – into thinking that psychology, both in its academic and psychotherapeutic guises, offers the best way to do it. Having heard nothing of Marx throughout their training, they become, like the philosophers he criticised, only interested in interpreting the world rather than seeking to directly intervene in it and change it.

The Mental Health System: Theory

The argument advanced in these pages is that the mental health system plays a pivotal role in shoring up the basic psychological processes which underpin acceptance of the capitalist system. To understand this one must first appreciate that the so-called science at the roots of the mental health system is flimsy in the extreme. The basic categories of mental disorder which are laid out in the DSM – the psychiatric Bible – have not been arrived at through painstaking scientific research, but through the operation of committees. Worse still the operation of these committees has been thoroughly corrupted by the influence of the pharmaceutical industry. Strong financial ties have been documented to exist between the industry and those who are responsible for developing and modifying the diagnostic criteria for mental illnesses. For example every single one of the panel members who met to decide on the criteria for mood disorders and schizophrenia had financial ties to drug companies. It has been suggested that over half of the members of all DSM committees had links with the pharmaceutical industry (Cosgrove et al., 2006).

The profession which adjudicates on what is or is not a mental illness has in the past decreed homosexuality to be a disease – a decision only rescinded under political protest by the gay community – and suggested masturbation leads to insanity. It is one which invented 'drapetomania' as a supposed mental illness that caused black slaves to flee captivity. It is a profession which has made stealing a disease (kleptomania) rather than a motivated behaviour. It is a profession which medicalises the painful responses of women to the disciplining pressures of the global fashion and food industries to conform, despite being under constant psychological, social and visual scrutiny. Indeed all genders must now constantly watch their weight and check their physical appearance for signs of lack of control, rather than seek any controls on the rampaging industries which dictate, in the name of profit, how we should look, feel, act, think and eat. The human body is now a conflict zone – a site where campaigns are fought with huge financial outlays inducing us to simultane-ously consume to excess and to regulate the effect of this consumption on our body. We are exhorted to change through physical fitness regimes, membership of sports clubs and gymna-siums, not to mention psychotherapy which can be bought and sold on the open market. This economic system is of course routinely ignored in any psychological analysis of 'dysfunctional' behaviour. Psychological housekeeping is to be promoted and preferred to consciousness-raising and organised political protest against predatory capitalist enterprises. We can even see signs in hospitals stating "Your health is your responsibility."

In more recent times we have also seen Post-Traumatic Stress Disorder (PTSD) invented as a means to appease Vietnam veterans who were lobbying for the right to receive benefits after returning shocked, ravaged and distressed from the imperial war in South-East Asia. PTSD itself is a particularly interesting example of psychiatric/psychological classification. Earlier volumes of the DSM declared that an essential feature of the 'disorder' was "a set of characteristic symptoms following a psychologically distressing event that is outside the usual range of human experience and that would be markedly distressing to almost anyone" (see APA, 1987, pp.247-51). The major problem with this is that the DSM also declares that a mental disorder by definition "must not be merely an expectable and culturally sanctioned response to a particular event" (p.xxxi). The 'PTSD' responses which one exhibits, then, are simultaneously to be considered a disease on the basis of the logic that they result from experiences which would be markedly distressing to anyone and at the same time not a disease because logically such responses should be expected given what people have experienced. No wonder then that former lead editor of the DSM Allen Francis declared there was no satisfactory definition of a mental disorder and that those which have been offered are "bullshit." Francis said, "you just can't define it" (cited in Greenberg, 2011). Francis' calls have recently been echoed by The National Institute of Mental Health (NIMH), the largest funder of psychiatric research, which has announced it will no longer support the DSM because "it lacks validity" and is "unscientific" (Insel, 2013). If expectable responses to unpleasant events should not be considered mental disorders then that would remove at a stroke virtually everything that is contained within the DSM.

Those clinical psychologists unimpressed by the nonsense which has prevailed in the mental health system since its inception have a clear understanding that, should one subtract those people from the mental health system who have been the unwitting recipients of or witnesses to emotional trauma, sexual and physical violence, neglect, bullying, intimidation and mystifying patterns of communication, there would be nobody left. PTSD occupies a crucial place in the mental health system precisely because it effectively implies that the class of persons it demarcates, and these only, have difficulties which pertain to what they have experienced. By implication all the other six hundred plus categories of mental disorder do not arise as consequences of the treatment life dishes out. As such the diagnosis of PTSD shores up the rest of the system: a system containing a phantasmagoria of conceptual categories, often indistinguishable from one another. These categories, almost in their entirety, lack any biological tests of validity i.e. there is no independent scientific evidence for the existence of the entities purportedly described other than the descriptions themselves. The reasoning is circular. Added to which, the diagnostic categories for the most part exhibit poor reliability – by which is meant mental health practitioners cannot decide with any consistency who does or doesn't have them. The problem can be well illustrated by the case of schizophrenia, which barely half the psychiatrists schooled in the medicalisation of behaviour for years on end actually believe in. It is a hypothetical disorder for which no tests exist, and professionals cannot agree on who has it. Accordingly this means that it has no greater scientific status than the zombie plague.

The upshot of all this is that diagnoses of mental illnesses are unscientific and are in fact never made for scientific reasons; their use is always driven by non-medical factors, whether they be economic, personal, legal, political or social. An instructive example of how social, legal and political factors have always been at the heart of the mental health system is revealed by the origin of the insanity defence used in criminal cases: the notion that someone can be excused their actions because they were not of sound mind (*non-compos mentis*) at the time they were committed. This can be traced back to the 17th century when suicide was defined as self-murder. Those sitting in judgement of the deceased were charged with punishing them, which in practice required them to dispossess the suicide's dependents of all available means of support and to desecrate the corpse of the deceased. This was at a time when industrialisation was rapidly spreading; people were moving into the towns and cities in increasing numbers and coroners and juries were being increasingly called on to act on the basis of these laws. Understandably as they became more and more uncomfortable at doing so it was they who sought to reform the law. As Szasz notes, "their religious beliefs precluded repeal of the laws punishing the crime. Their only recourse was to evade the laws: The doctrine that the self-slayer is *non-compos mentis* and hence not responsible for his act accomplished this" (2007b, p.99). This legal evasion permitted what was morally unacceptable –punishment of the innocent – to be revoked while maintaining the religious and legal status quo. No scientific evidence has ever been produced to support the current legal position that essentially anti-social and undesirable acts are produced by those of unsound mind. People who harm themselves or harm others have not been shown to have diseased brains or minds, whatever that could mean. The notion is a legal fiction reified through three centuries of practice into an assumed truth.

The unscientific nature of mental health diagnoses aside, they have the deleterious consequence of inducing social divisions and social rejection; that is they are the cause of stigma toward those designated as mentally ill. Abnormal psychology and psychiatry presupposes there to be two classes of people: the mentally healthy and the mentally ill. The mentally healthy are effectively those 'best' adapted to living in an extreme capitalist society, who can withstand or participate in the exploitation of others without a sign of personal protest or emotional distress. Those who sit at the top of the capitalist tree by contrast appear incapable of feeling much at all – certainly not compassion for those who pay the greatest price for their accumulation of obscene amounts of wealth. It is no accident that definitions of mental health which have previously been offered in the behavioural sciences include "the ability to maintain an even temper" and the absence of "industrial unrest" (see Clare, 1980, p.15). Indeed anger is arguably the most pathologised emotion of all – not surprisingly when it is the emotion most needed to bring about constructive change. The regulation of so-called abnormal behaviour has always been about the maintenance of the status quo. Consequently it is no surprise that the majority of the clients/patients who file through the mental health system queues come from groups who bear the brunt of this savage status quo. Whilst raw power and material interest have continued to exert a strong influence on the lives of people, they have not featured in psychological thinking about mental health – or indeed anything else. It is hard to see this as accidental.

The function of psychology and psychiatry within the capitalist system is firstly to expand the category of the mentally ill thereby creating customers for pharmacological interventions (about which more shortly) and to create fear in the so-called 'mentally healthy' that they may fall into the latter category at a moment's notice. To recap, theory states that the mentally ill are in that category because of some pre-existing biological/medical vulnerability. No wonder then that the public has learnt to fear them. This seems an entirely rational response to being told that there are people out in the world who have no control over their actions and who may spring at barely a moment's notice into some disturbed pattern of behaviour on the basis of some biologically driven clockwork imperative uninfluenced by motive or volition. After all, we are told, psychiatric 'illness' is just like any other 'illness.' Except of course it is not. One telling indicator of this is that the advances in knowledge in physical medicine, which deals with real diseases, have over the last century been routine. In psychiatry which deals with fake socially constructed illnesses they have been non-existent.

The second function of the mental health industry – and this flows logically from the first – is that it serves purposes of social control. It is well known that dissidents in the former Soviet Empire were dispatched to the Gulag with all manner of pseudo-scientific psychiatric diagnoses, 'sluggish schizophrenia' being one of the more popular ones. Likewise service personnel who have questioned what they were doing thousands of miles from home being asked to kill Argentine or Iraqi men with whom they have no personal quarrel have similarly been referred to psychiatric services. Philippe Petit's (2002) account of his high-wire walk across the twin towers of the World Trade Centre in 1974 is also illuminating. After performing his "artistic crime of the century" Petit was arrested and interviewed by psychiatrists. Why was this? What had his unconventional behaviour to do with medicine? Petit – an imaginative, unusual and beguiling figure – exemplifies much that modern psychiatry stands against. According to his autobiography, Petit cares not for the rules and regulations which structure and govern the lives of citizens. He lives, in his terms, to dream "projects that ripen in the clouds" (p.6). The mental health system is an enterprise that seeks to destroy these for it cannot tolerate idiosyncrasies of thought, whether grandiose or mundane, whether overtly political or not. The mental health system teaches us to fear our own thoughts, to keep within the straight and narrow of acceptable thought; it teaches us to fear the unconventional, to abhor alternative ways of being and experiencing the world, to psychologise conflict, to call those we disagree with mad, to substitute pseudo-medical diagnosis for contemplation, argument and debate. In doing so it restricts our notions of what it means to be human and turns us against ourselves. Marx's own personal maxim, stated to his daughter Jenny, came from the ancient Roman playwright Terence: "*Nihil humani a me alienum puto,*" or, "nothing human can be alien to me" (cited in Fromm, 2011, p.257). We need to cultivate and disseminate such sentiments.

The Mental Health System: Practice

If we contemplate the role and purpose of the mental health system in practice, we must perforce contend with another layer of mystification. If we are in dire straits, or somebody we care for is, our immediate need is for the system to 'fix' the problem: to return us to 'normal' functioning; to a stable equilibrium of serenity and well-being in the face of everything. To live well is of course possible, but the primary aim of the mental health system is not to do this. The major interventions on offer – be they pharmacological (drugs), electrical (ECT: electro convulsive therapy) or in extreme cases surgical (leucotomy/lobotomy) – for the most part are intended to eliminate emotions, dangerous freedoms excised for peaceful slavery. The major predictable effects of the interventions are to tranquilise, to sedate, to calm: to reduce the person in difficulty to a more compliant state where they are more 'manageable' and less of a nuisance. Suitably decontaminated of their nuisance generating potential, the aberrant person can then be returned as 'fit' to the workplace – should any jobs actually still exist in the dysfunctional capitalist economy. The advent of IAPT (improved access to psychological therapies) which seeks to make CBT (cognitive-behaviour therapy) more widely and quickly available is similarly designed to get people back to work in the shortest space of time. The improved access really means improved access to exploitative work and is not specifically designed to get people to function well in either their private or public lives.

One of the myths surrounding the predominant form of intervention – drugs – is that, whether they are called anti-depressants, anxiolytics (anti-anxiety) or anti-psychotics, they are well formulated, scientifically developed agents which specifically target well-understood disease processes. Nothing could be further from the truth. It needs to be widely understood that there is no good evidence whatsoever of any biological defect or chemical imbalance in anybody who presents with extreme unhappiness, anxiety or disturbed behaviour. This is a widely disseminated myth propagated by drug companies and uncritically endorsed and disseminated by both the media and significant numbers of the academic community. The fact is that the evidence base for the putative efficacy of these different classes of drugs rests on extremely poor science. In thorough analyses both Joanna Moncrieff (2008) and Irvin Kirsch (2009) have systematically unmasked the claims on which the sale of these drugs trade. Kirsch for example, focusing on the use of anti-depressants, shows not only that the quality of drug trials sponsored by the Big Pharma corporations leave something to be desired, but that the extent of the supposed gains displayed by patients in trials correlates very highly with the magnitude of the side effects which the drugs produce. In short the poor quality of the trials enables patients to guess – even in a supposed double blind trial – which condition, placebo or active drug, they are actually in. A person can correctly guess on the basis that they are experiencing side effects that they are in the active drug condition. The more the side effects, the greater the accuracy of the guess. Having deduced that, they are then prone to all manner of expectancy effects, such that they will have greater confidence that the drugs will work. Given that anti-depressants are supposed to relieve feelings of depression and they are now taking part in a clinical trial, it is fairly logical (though mistaken) for the participants in the trials to believe that what they are being given will make them feel better.

Kirsch also goes further than demystifying the bogus claims of the multinationals. In an epilogue to his book he writes what many in the business know but few dare to say: that the research merry-go-round is kept on the road by coercion and threats to academic staff to toe the line, and that failure to do so can quickly lead to job loss and career implosion. In summary, a false set of beliefs and an ideological stance kept in place by force of money, bad science and threats is a view which finds echoes in Ian Parker's work. His contention is that psychology constitutes "a fascinating ideological system and coercive apparatus for normalising and pathologising behaviour and experience" and that "all the elements of alienation and reification that characterise capitalism are condensed in [it]" (cited in Hepburn, 2003, p.47). The 'psy' professions as Parker calls them have revelled in the pretension that they can usefully tell us how to live well or in a way which is 'mentally healthy.' Backed up by media psychologists, agony aunts and an assortment of gurus and experts this lie has gained considerable credence. This cult of expert nonsense must be resisted, through hard work, commitment to the truth and to one another and appreciation of the short-lived joys that life can offer in the struggle ahead. The solutions to our ills are organic not technical. The psychology bandwagon ultimately offers only technical solutions – those which serve the surveillance and control needs/demands of an authoritarian if not totalitarian industrial society.

In the final chapter we will begin a somewhat different discussion of how one's life (and the lives of others) can be improved. Kirsch, unusually for a psychologist, on the final page of his examination of the drug industry argued that if we are to do so "we need to change the social conditions – such as racism, unemployment, poverty, unaffordable housing and lack of adequate education – that put people at increased risk of" mental health conditions (2009, p.136). The list might also usefully include patriarchy. This view, one which is undoubtedly correct, warrants a central place in the discipline.

Chapter 4

Psychology and Militarism

War is a racket. It always has been. It is possibly the oldest, easily the most profitable, surely the most vicious. It is the only one international in scope. It is the only one in which the profits are reckoned in dollars and the losses in lives... It is conducted for the benefit of the very few, at the expense of the very many. Out of war a few people make huge fortunes.
(Smedley, D. Butler, 1935)[5]

Prior to the Global War on Terror, detention facilities and intelligence operations used indigenous assets to accomplish their missions. Often, these intelligence units lacked the resources of a well-trained operational psychologist. In fact most intelligence units did not have a psychologist assigned to its unit. However as the operational tempo in Iraq and Afghanistan escalated, an increase in the number of detainees and military detention facilities increased as well. As a result, within a short period of time, the need for psychologists from other parts of the DOD to serve as Behavioural Science Consultants (BSCs) drastically increased.
(James & Pulley, 2013, p.158)

Psychology, War and the Military-Industrial Complex

War is easily misunderstood. Its attractions exist at many levels. For those who directly participate in it, it can give great meaning and purpose, can create a sense of being a part of history and therefore something greater than what one feels in the ordinary course of day to day affairs; it can forge unbreakable bonds with friends and comrades, can create an addictive allure for those who have been too often but a second away from having their life snuffed out. But that isn't even half the story. Those who participate in war are rarely those who make it. Its attractions probably operate most strongly amongst those who draw political resolve, fame, power and just cause from the 'necessity' to engage with it. Chris Hedges described it as an "enticing elixir" (2002, p.5), former Conservative Defence Minister, Alan Clark, as an "intoxicating brew" (cited in Curtis, 1995). Clark also went on to say that once politicians had enjoyed a taste of this brew they did not know when to stop. Both Churchill and Thatcher he opined were drunk on it. The same, it might also be said, goes for the discipline of psychology which has been sitting at the bar with the defence industry for decades.

The biggest attraction of war however, it has long been argued, is not just for combatants, or those caught up in its mayhem, or the politicians who revel in its glory, but for the capitalist system. This perspective holds that capitalism needs war to renew itself, to expand its sponsors' reach into new untapped markets, and to gain access to and control of cheap raw materials (see Nitzan & Bichler, 2006). The Gulf War in 1991 for example yielded estimated profits of between 50 and 150 billion dollars (Gittings, 1991) while the 2003 Iraq War saw the oil company Halliburton bring home profits of close to 40 billion dollars. Halliburton is typical; the wars in both Vietnam and the Middle East have been of great benefit for the major oil companies and arms contractors. Support for war and the industries that nurture it is on this account support for the system that profits from it and arguably encourages it to reap those profits. One might think that this would be a suitable topic for the new disciple of political psychology. Phil Banyard had it about right when he wrote "if there is to be an impact on psychology (of the war in Iraq), then hopefully it will encourage us to describe and understand why groups of people decide to wreak havoc on civilian populations for political ends, and to help develop forums for dissent that are peaceful and constructive" (2004, p.624). Alas no, the behaviour of elites in government and business – and increasingly these are one and the same – have seldom attracted the interests of psychologists. Accordingly political psychology has already, for the most part, retreated into a sterile preoccupation with the abstract cognitive basis of decision-making in political contexts. Wikipedia describes its aims as "to understand interdependent relationships between individuals and contexts that are influenced by beliefs, motivation, perception, cognition, information processing, learning strategies, socialization and attitude formation"[6]. This is almost a recipe for the studied neglect of what is actually important: the politics of psychology and its interface with the military-industrial complex. When it comes to political decisions which have adverse consequences, it resembles nothing so much as the search for original sin.

Psychology's regular stance toward the purveyors of war is best illustrated by an examination of British Psychology's institutional response to the war in Iraq in 2003. Outside the cosy confines of the US military and the psychologists embedded within it, the operations in Iraq – the invasion of a sovereign country – were widely understood to be war crimes; indeed that was the position taken by the then Secretary General of the UN, Kofi Annan. The war of course, as does any war, had a number of pertinent psychological issues: how players in the theatre of war understand their own actions, the Orwellian nature of the language utilised to justify military engagement, psychologists' roles in designing and orchestrating actions and propaganda, the physical and psychological damage/trauma to Iraqi citizens and combatants on all sides, the unquestioned assumptions about the benign nature and noble intent of British actions abroad, the corresponding increased fears of terrorist actions, civil chaos (here and in Iraq), xenophobia, repressive and totalitarian government, loss of civil liberties, issues of trust in the media and politicians, as well as the role of media coverage in influencing beliefs and understanding.

Despite this litany of relevant issues, the contents of the British Psychological Society's (BPS) in-house magazine during the first 21 months of the war had virtually nothing to say about it (Roberts, 2007). The very few brief mentions which were made in the media section of the magazine made it clear that the major interest in the war for the BPS appeared to be whether psychologists were appearing in the media! A lugubrious obsession with their own importance was further evidenced in January 2003 by an open invitation on the cover of *The Psychologist* for readers to "vote for your top psychologists." The result was announced while the war was in full swing and received a good deal more coverage than it. Comparative analyses of the contents of *The British Medical Journal* and *The Lancet* indicated a different response was possible. Both of these medical publications devoted considerable coverage to the war and its aftermath including the political and humanitarian aspects. In *The Lancet*, for example Rubenstein commented that "one of the perverse effects of the war on terrorism has been the revival of the idea that torture can be legitimate in so-called exceptional cases" (2003, p.1556). The BPS had nothing to say about the subject of torture for another two years and about its use in the Iraq War/War on Terror it has still said nothing.

The conclusions drawn from this exercise were not limited to the fact that British Psychology is selling itself as if it were nothing more than a brand of cornflakes nor that the Society's magazine has come to resemble a version of *Hello* magazine for behavioural scientists, but more significantly that the British Psychological Society's output conforms to Herman and Chomsky's (1994) propaganda model of the media. Chomsky and Herman argue that the media in the Western world serves a propaganda function in so far as information is presented (or not presented) in such a way so as to legitimise elite interests against the interests of the majority of the population. Psychology's institutional avoidance of any critical stance toward UK military involvement in Iraq seems to imply that any war the UK is engaged in is a just and necessary one. Its implicit agenda is arguably one in which its avowed concerns will be only those apolitical issues that satisfy the curiosity of the middle-class citizens of the world who have yet to confront the military reality of Anglo-American capitalism.

The mind-set of the military (and other) psychologists who subscribe to the West's right to deliver terror onto somebody else's doorstep can be an object lesson in alienation and mystification. James & Pulley, a quote from whose work opened this chapter, demonstrate that their own estrangement from basic humanitarian impulses has reached such a degree that they actually ask themselves in all seriousness whether the psychologist is a "health care professional or a clearly defined combatant" (p.160). If they reflect on this question a little more the answer may be instructive. That the American Psychological Association has felt itself unable to condemn outright the participation of its members in such activities perfectly demonstrates just how deeply ingrained the values of nationalism, militarism and imperialism have become. That such a profession dares to lecture students or anybody else for that matter on matters of objectivity bias and ethics must be considered not simply hypocritical but also surreal.

In addition to the widely judged illegality of the Iraq War, it was also understood as an attempt to gain control of Iraq's energy reserves for Western Companies. Of interest here again is James & Pulley's piece, which contains a brief section entitled "Ethical Issues." Participating in illegal international wars in order to gain control of a country's resources to bolster the capitalist economies of the West received no mention. Nor should we expect it to. Psychologists have been extensively schooled in filtering out the broader context within which people operate. Naturally enough this operation is also applied to themselves with predictable enough consequences. Maybe we can consider such self-duping to be one aspect of PSYOPS (psychological operations).

Psychological Operations

Psychological operations are used in many ways. The 'shock and awe' strategy of the 2003 Iraq War can be considered its most visible manifestation. The immense display of coalition fire power was designed at the outset to produce an attitude of resignation and defeat in both the Iraqi fighting forces and the civilian population. In Britain, the army maintains a psychological warfare unit: the 15 Psychological Operations group. The group, which was established shortly after the 1991 Gulf War comprises over 150 personnel, with around half of these drawn from the regular Armed Services and the other from the Reserves which may comprise people from the media, broadcasting and publishing. In addition there is GCHQ's "Human Science Operations Cell," in which psychologists are employed to train people to "not only understand, but shape and control, how online activism and discourse unfolds" (Greenwald, 2014). The intention is to destroy reputations and break up activist organisations. Internal documents from GCHQ acknowledge that this "online covert action" is primarily directed against "people who have *nothing to do with terrorism or national security threat*" (Global Research, 2014). While other countries also employ psychological operations it is the US military who make far more substantial use of them. Just a few examples are given below. Others are described at length by Harper (2007) and Rampton & Stauber (2003).

One of the most significant illustrations of the use of PSYOPS comes from the 1991 Gulf War. During this a story appeared which detailed how Iraqi soldiers had removed babies from incubators in Kuwait in October 1990. One of the chief 'witnesses' to this who testified before the US Congressional Human Rights Caucus was Nayirah, a 15-year-old Kuwaiti girl. Her tearful and convincing evidence was widely reported at the time. What was not reported was that she was the daughter of the Kuwaiti Ambassador to the US and her evidence had been coached by Lauri Fitz-Pegado, Vice President of Hill and Knowlton, one of the largest PR firms in the world (see Harper, 2007). Then consider the activities of PR consultant, John W. Rendon who worked on extensive Iraq-related activities under contract to the Pentagon and the CIA. His contribution to mass deception included responsibility for the distribution of flags bearing the colours of the US and other coalition countries to Kuwaiti residents. Rendon described himself as an "information warrior" and a "perception manager" (p.42), classically Orwellian terms for orchestrated lying. The Pentagon sees these terms slightly differently, defining perception management as the combination of "truth projection, operations security, cover and deception" (p.42). The use of "truth projection" and "deception" simultaneously clearly indicates it is not truth which is being projected!

Perhaps the most well-known example however of manipulating the public through "perception management" and deception is the infamous claim made in The UK prior to the 2003 invasion that Iraq had Weapons of Mass Destruction (WMD) able to be deployed within 45 minutes. Although Secretary of State Colin Powell, only 2 years earlier, had pronounced Saddam posed no threat and had been contained[7], this inconvenient truth was utterly ignored in favour of a PR campaign using psychological operations techniques to elevate the perceived threat felt by the general public, to curtail weapons inspections by the UN, and to bolster the case for war. Part of the "truth projection" coming out of Downing Street originated from the so-called dodgy dossier: a 12-years-old uncited PhD thesis downloaded from the Internet. Psychological operations are today just one part of a comprehensive relationship between psychology and the military. So great is this relationship that it has become a sub-discipline of psychology in its own right.

Military Psychology

Psychology has a long history of engagement with the military. Toward the end of the First World War a committee from the US National Research Council proposed that psychologists be commissioned as active duty officers. The President of the American Psychological Association, Robert Yerkes, was amongst the first to be recruited. Before long, psychologists were involved in personnel selection and the training of aviation crew (Hopewell, 2013). This was quickly followed by the use of intelligence tests by the US Army (these are now widely acknowledged to have been racist), research on propaganda, leadership and group dynamics, perception, instrument design and ergonomics. By the time World War Two had finished, the explicit application of psychology for military purposes had been consolidated in the US into the emergent discipline of military psychology. This encompassed everything from selection and training, propaganda, leadership, personal adjustment and mental health care (dealing with for example combat stress/shell shock and sleep disorders), neuropsychology, psychopharmacology, soldier fitness and hostage negotiation to the relationship of personality to military service. The latter provides an instructive example of psychological myopia. In a discussion of soldier motivation to enlist, De Vries and Wijnans (2013) for example devote some attention to the personality trait of conscientiousness (one of the supposed Big Five factors which make up the core of human personality) and its potential role in the decisions of young men and women to join the armed services and fulfil their sense of duty. While they do this they fail miserably to contemplate the role of other factors in enlistment: the poor state of the US economy, the dominant role played by the military in the industrial landscape of America and the nationalist indoctrination that is ubiquitous in the educational and media environments young people have to traverse. Subsequent imperial wars in Korea, Vietnam, and the Middle East have seen continued strengthening of the relationship between psychologists, psychological knowledge and military activity. In passing it can be said that this provides an exemplary illustration of Foucault's thesis of the intertwining of power and knowledge.

The quote which opens this chapter neatly illustrates a good deal of the problem inherent with psychologists' involvement with the military-industrial complex. Nowhere in it, nor indeed in the chapter from which it was taken – one contained in Moore & Barnett's *Military Psychologists' Desk Reference* – is there any questioning of exactly what is meant by the phrase they use: "the operational tempo in Iraq and Afghanistan" (2013, p.158). The realities of this "tempo" – the mass murder, bombing, maiming, torture, misery, destruction of life, limb and property – like so much else in capitalist economics, do not occupy any rows or columns on the invading army's balance sheet nor do they seem to find a place in the conscience of the many psychologists whose efforts the war machine depends on. One of the few pieces of psychological research to gain wide currency outside of academia was Milgram's (1974) work on obedience to authority. The stark message to come out of Milgram's work was that a good many people were prepared to do almost anything when asked to do so by what they considered to be a 'legitimate' authority. Milgram was at pains to point out that not all authority was legitimate; seemingly in his experiment this could include the authority of psychology and of science. That psychology and the national military organisations that fund it to do work on behalf of governments and defence contractors – multinational corporations who make profit from death – might also not be legitimate authorities has never been contemplated in any mainstream academic psychology journal that I am aware of.

As ever psychology comes in handy for diverting attention away from economic or structural causes of human behaviour. Its capacity to do this is of course just one of the reasons why it is greeted so enthusiastically in the corridors of power. Faced with the enormity and grave nature of the world situation it is too easy to blame the 'original sin' of the human character and lapse into hopelessness while the historical-structural nature of our predicament escapes scrutiny. In a rare critical examination of the presuppositions which underpin psychology, David Smail contends that it is the "societal operation of power and interest" which is of immeasurably greater importance when it comes to understanding human conduct, much more than anything that may reside in our personal psychology (2005, p.21). Why this seems so hard for us to accept owes much to the fact that the great sources of power in our lives – economics, politics, culture and ideology – are physically remote from us, while the lesser sources of power – education, family and workplace for example – are situated literally right in front of our noses. The illusion that psychology is really more important than it actually is can be compared to the error in judging a ten pence coin to be bigger than the sun simply because we have placed it a small distance in front of our eyes.

Unbeknown to most people who work in the discipline, psychology's close relationship with the military has shaped its development to a considerable degree. While psychoanalysts saw in the Second World War an opportunity to promote their profession in lieu of the challenges posed by the escalating numbers of psychologically scarred veterans returning from the battlefields of Europe, it was academic psychology which was shaped by its close involvement with the military, not only during the Second World War but also throughout the Cold War. Its present-day status owes much to the extensive close links which were developed during these times. The military's requirement for measurable technologies to assess human performance influenced not only the early use of IQ tests; it also helped cement a specifically quantifiable approach to attitudes and personality. Eysenck's factor analytic work on personality for example grew out of the treatment of psychologically damaged soldiers. Yet this is a largely fruitless approach which has yielded little beyond its propensity to pigeonhole and categorise people. Game theory which occupies a key theoretical place in social psychology was likewise a product of the RAND Corporation's strategists dreaming up nuclear nightmare scenarios. The aptly named Mutually Assured Destruction (MAD) was just one of these. Given psychology's entanglement with the aims and goals of war-fighting nations, it becomes easier to see why so much of the way psychology is practiced (some might say 'performed') concurs with a capitalist ethos. Nowhere is this more apparent than in the growth and development of cognitive psychology.

Psychology, War and Memory

The predominant views of the human organism in psychology have always owed much to the metaphors we draw from the latest technological developments. In the 1930s the brain was likened to a gigantic telephone switchboard, a view that was consigned to history with the development of digital computers. Now the information-processing metaphor reigns supreme and the brain is considered to be a sophisticated biological computer; research work to interface digital hardware with the soft tissue of the brain is well under way. The age of the cyborg is almost upon us. This presupposes a view of memory which has profound implications for how the world we live in unfolds. In the heat of the Cold War and the age of nuclear terror, mutual fear, deception and paranoia, the basis of our consensual reality seemed increasingly open to uncertainty, doubt and question. Because of this, memory assumed particular importance. Research sought to determine how malleable memory was, to what degree it could be externally programmed and controlled and whether the traces of such attempted programming could be erased. In many ways the work on the constructive nature of memory undermined completely the notion that one could distinguish true from false memories solely on the basis of their content. The legacy of this is in many ways the nightmare world envisioned in the novels of Philip K. Dick. It is also our world in the 21st century.

The political desire to control human memory, to erase it almost completely and to be able to 'install' a new personality malleable to political expedient, was the basis for the little known but horrific experiments of the Canadian psychiatrist Ewen Cameron and his colleague Lloyd H. Cotter (readers potentially uncomfortable with the details of this might wish to skip the next two paragraphs). This political wish coincided with the psychotherapeutic one which saw people's problems as rooted in their past experience. The psychotherapeutic wish merged with the capitalist prerogative for quick simple marketable solutions and so Cameron convinced himself that CIA money was a force for good. While Cameron's motivation was arguably rooted in his psychiatric upbringing, the CIA's desire was to produce trained amoral assassins who would do literally anything without compunction. The cultural recollection of these CIA-funded assaults on human dignity, just one part of their MKUltra psychological research program, lives on through such films as *The Manchurian Candidate* and the *Bourne* films. Cameron instituted a 'treatment' regime involving a process he termed depatterning. In practice what this meant for his patients was drug induced coma for up to 86 days, followed by ECT three times daily with finally "a football helmet clamped to the head for up to twenty-one days with a looped tape repeating, up to half a million times, messages like 'my mother hates me'" (McCoy, 2006, p.44).

Cotter then attempted "under field conditions" to assess how Cameron's depatterning techniques would work. In a hospital north of Saigon, Cotter instituted a mass operant conditioning experiment whereby patients who wanted to leave were told they must work for three months "to prove their capability" (1967, p.24). This involved tending crops for American Special Forces troops in Viet Cong territory. Those refusing (over 90 per cent of the patients) received unmodified ECT (i.e. ECT without tranquillisers or muscle relaxants). This was continued at the rate of three times a week until the patient's behaviour was deemed to be improved. When a similar procedure failed on a second ward – after seven weeks – food was withdrawn until, after three further days, all of the 130 female patients 'volunteered' for work. These 'recovered' patients were subsequently given duties which involved working in Special Forces camps prone to attack by the Viet Cong.

The association between psychology and the defence industries however continued despite the failure of Cameron's research to deliver what had been hoped for. Warped by Cold War dynamics, Cameron's work had found that controlling the dark forces of history was beyond a simple matter of memory control. A century earlier Nietzsche warned that "whoever fights monsters should see to it that in the process he does not become a monster" (2003, p.102). The warning was not heeded, as warnings seldom are. Instead psychology and behavioural science in general duly became those dark forces. Two distinct murky fields were duly ploughed. By the time the CIA pulled the plug on these ventures, several of the key behavioural components of torture had been established: sensory deprivation, self-inflicted pain and obedience to authority (McCoy, 2006). These formed the basis for the application of psychological torture in Northern Ireland and later Iraq and Afghanistan which came to be known collectively as the 'five techniques': hooding, noise bombardment, food deprivation, sleep deprivation and forced standing. Cognitive psychologist Tim Shallice observed that "psychologists by investigating the nature of brainwashing have improved it" (1972, p.387). Shallice also argued that psychologists had a special responsibility for some of the interrogation techniques used by the British military which appear to have been derived by the "conscious use of available scientific knowledge" (p.387).

In a similar fashion US psychologists contributed to the development of a range of 'enhanced' interrogation techniques, among them 'waterboarding,' a technique which makes breathing extremely difficult for those being interrogated and reliably produces states of extreme tension where the person will fear imminent death by asphyxiation. The 'Behavioral Science Consultation Teams' deployed in Iraq at Abu Ghraib were given authorisation to use these techniques. Psychologists were fully paid-up members of them. In fact psychology's complicity with torture is no better illustrated than the recent refusal of the American Psychological Association (APA) to pursue ethics charges against psychologist John Leso. Official documents implicate Leso in the "enhanced interrogation" techniques used at Guantánamo Bay (Brody, 2014; see also PHR, 2010). Furthermore the APA does not dispute Leso's role in the interrogation of detainee Mohammed Al-Qahtani in which Al-Qahtani was hooded, leashed and treated like a dog, subject to sleep deprivation, sexual humiliation, prolonged exposure to cold, forced nudity and sustained isolation. Despite Al-Qahtani's treatment meeting the legal definition of torture the APA decided there was "nothing unethical about Leso's actions" (Brody, 2014).

The CIA's malign influence on the discipline, sadly, does not stop at brainwashing and torture. According to John Marks (Assistant to CIA Director of Intelligence and Research) the "CIA funded perhaps 15 and 20 key people right across the fields of psychology and brain research" (in Curtis, 1995). The intention was to dictate the direction of research in these fields for years to come. As such, says Marks, "the CIA played a catalytic role in the development of psychology as we know it today" (Curtis, 1995). Many of those funded of course deny their involvement. The direction which psychology then predominantly took, even in those areas which are supposedly concerned with our social behaviour, has been cognitive. Since the 1960s cognitive psychology has been driven by the goal of producing artificial intelligence: to understand the human mind sufficiently well that its basic operating principles, decision-making prowess and memory abilities could be instantiated into a machine. Much of this work has been funded by the military, a fact seldom discussed in university departments awed by the philosophical problems of consciousness and machine intelligence. The question of what role our emotions play in life has always been considered of secondary importance – if it has been considered at all, which it rarely has.

With the influence of the CIA and the defence industries on research, psychology has often resembled a morality-free zone. This is another fact well camouflaged by the attention given to ethics in undergraduate degree courses. Most psychological research for the military meanwhile remains classified and unpublished, and with the defence industry the largest employer of psychologists, the vast majority of the work they do remains out of sight. But what *is* the nature of the work they do? In addition to torture assistance, it may perhaps be summarised under the headings of: 1) the construction of intelligent weapons systems; 2) selection of personnel not morally troubled by fighting and killing or operating the machinery of war; 3) psychological operations to pacify 'hostile' domestic and international targets; and 4) the development of surveillance technology.

Psychologists like to kid themselves that working on such topics as image processing, speech recognition, face recognition, thinking and programmable memory belong in the realm of pure science even as the hardware encapsulating all these capacities rolls off the production lines of gigantic defence corporations. That this has almost nothing to do with the Enlightenment dreams of human reason propelling life in a continually progressive and benign direction has somehow escaped the attention of the profession. The noted psychologist Jerome Bruner when interviewed described the Panglossian mentality of many of his colleagues in this respect as naïve and characterised by a kind of "magical thinking" that the Big Brother society they were helping to bring about would somehow turn out to be benign (Curtis, 1995).

Thus psychologists remain not merely in denial – an internal recognition perhaps that the state of the world and the abuses of power within it, which they contribute to, are too widespread and terrible to contemplate (Cohen, 2001) – but also in a state of self-hypnosis, one which increasingly echoes the robotic, emotionally unreflective awareness of the machinery they create for the security state and the military-industrial complex. The apotheoses of their intellectual achievement are the cruise missile and the unmanned drones which circle the skies of Pakistan and other countries inhabited by poor people killing civilians by the score. We are aided and abetted in avoiding thinking about the real implications of all this for a number of reasons. There is the preponderance of an awestruck attitude to science; a corresponding gee-whizz fascination with the complexities of advanced technology; not to forget a global film industry, whose conveyor belt sci-fi output consistently and effectively blurs the boundaries between fantasy and reality to an extent that anything is simultaneously believable and unbelievable – an aide to the plausible deniability which is a central plank in the world of *realpolitik*. It cannot be denied that psychology's long association with authority and power, from the perspective of those who wield it and wish to maintain it, has been fruitful. It also begs the question of what controls professional societies are effectively able to exert over military psychologists when so much of what they do is carried out in secret. Then there is the question of whether the relationship between psychology and the military is a healthy one for the rest of society. The contention within these pages is that it is not and we need to get wise while we still can.

Chapter 5

Psychology, Business and the Market

A possible reason why some businessmen are willing to tolerate a psychologist underfoot is that they may have made a good profit by following his advice.
(Miller, 1966, p.20)

The persuasion industry is increasingly powerful, but if you consider yourself immune to its blandishments – if you think that as a consumer, everything you buy is the result of your own free will – take a look around your possessions.
(Lewis, 2013, p.1)

Introduction

Travel broadens the mind, so it is said. Alas, depending on the mind-set which accompanies one's adventures, it may also narrow it. There is no doubt however that exposure to a different way of life at least offers the potential for one to question customary habits and cultural mores. Spending time in the wilderness or at least in some of the more inaccessible places of the planet Earth invariably throws up at least one startling contrast to life in our urban and cultural bolt holes. Whether wandering through the metropolis, listening to the radio, surfing the TV channels or browsing the World Wide Web, one may discover at least one activity that appears ubiquitous – the never-ending attempt to sell us something. Along with this capitalist universal is the desire to transform and reduce human consciousness to a primitive compulsion to buy. Everyone it seems wants to sell us something – anything in fact.

We are no longer the knowing species (sapiens) but the devouring one (consume). We can no longer remember a time when life was any different. Naomi Klein's (2010) critique of the excesses of unfettered capitalism, *No Logo*, opens with a studied elaboration of the extent of this phenomenon. She recognises that the spaces – both physical and mental – where we can escape the onslaught of capitalism are vanishingly few and decreasing in size. Everywhere, 24/7, we are regaled with an unceasing flow of corporate brands, celebrity endorsements, visual, aural, tactile and olfactory displays of the latest must-have throwaway products, designed to drive us relentlessly on, to spend without limit or care. Much of this revolves around our own wish to make temporarily good our fragile self-esteem, which has, in the first place, been damaged by the creation, manufacture and distribution of personal deficit, failing and status. Capitalism feeds off this endless cycle of created needs and needless wants to keep itself afloat. Beyond the satisfaction of life's necessities it is not hard to see that the imperatives to consume have a distinctly psychological character. After all it is our motivations, desires, hopes and feelings – all of the utmost personal nature – which are subject to the manipulative exhortations of the corporate behemoth.

Contrary to received wisdom, the dynamics of consumerism are not a blind force of nature, an indication of some tragic flaw in the human character[8], but the result of a perfectly understandable self-perpetuating social and economic system. To function anything like as effectively as it has done, the black art and 'science' of selling things has come to rely on a sizeable input from psychologists. In the process of aiding and abetting the expansion of capitalist values into every nook and cranny of existence, psychology too has been changed. The traffic has not been one-way. This is probably most evident when we consider the issue of marketing. Decades of psychological input to this have resulted not only in the colonisation of public space, with its concomitant erosion of the personal and communal, but an ever-expanding field of 'goods' to populate the social field. In the maelstrom psychology too has found itself branded, another perishable product to flash before the eyes of prospective buyers.

This is explicable in part by the nature of the corporate managerial habitat which psychology resides in. With higher education commoditised, psychology is simply another product on the supermarket shelf. Unlike a good many others however which manage to maintain a modicum of self-respect, psychology is oblivious to resistance and celebrates its self–abasement and unconditional surrender to selling itself on the open market; its blandishments for establishment tastes range from the truly obscene to the terrifyingly banal. At the obscene end of the spectrum we have psychologists touting for business, offering to improve the efficiency of state security and surveillance as well as to demonise political protesters and opponents of imperialist conquest as terrorists and psychologically disturbed. In one sense its primary 'product' on offer could be considered a part of the service industry, the service on offer being to rebrand social, political and economic problems as psychological ones. Because of this, the psychologisation of the world functions as a political tool to fracture the forces of social cohesion which resist the onslaught of the profit motive. For example, rather than conflict in the Middle East, the growth of Islamic fundamentalism, the War on Islam, the War on Terror, climate change and opposition to fracking being framed as common consequences of an industrial 'addiction' to fossil fuels (and the power of multinational oil companies), psychology instead envisages the social *consequences* as fundamental and seeks mysterious hidden psychological operations such as 'identity processes' and 'threat management' to explain the appearance of the social world (see for example Jaspal & Coyle, in press; Jaspal & Nerlich, in press; Jaspal, Nerlich & Cinnirella, 2014; Nerlich & Jaspal, in press). Psychology thus literally turns the world inside out. A service for the rich and a disservice to everyone else!

At the banal end of the continuum psychologists can be found prostrate before advertising executives, guns for hire to assist big business to lie and deceive with aplomb; all in order that the public says goodbye to its money for an indefinite number of useless, worthless and unneeded products. In the corporate middle-ground they can be found helping Big Pharma to push its unwanted and on occasion dangerous products onto a sceptical public. Underlying these various tales of subservience is an unstated and implicit ideological position (see Chapter 2). In addition however there is increasingly an explicit theoretical basis to the provision of psychological services to the market. Broadly speaking these can be grouped under three main headings: the psychology of marketing, behavioural economics and business psychology. Whilst these are sufficiently different to warrant distinct discussions of each – which we will proceed to do here – it is also useful to appreciate that in one way or another they all have a major preoccupation with the art and science of persuasion and ultimately lend spurious scientific cover to a project of political economy.

Classical economics, rooted in the ideas of Adam Smith, is predicated on the notion of a free market in which the buyer has perfect information about the utility, availability and need regarding the products on offer. This perfect field of information surrounding a 'good' should of course also address the future consequences of its use. As is well known, this is a fiction (see Dietz, 2011), not to mention the habit engrained in classical economics to externalise costs and consequences. In one sense, one might argue that advertising functions to fill this informational vacuum by notifying potential customers about the existence of certain products, their properties and functions. But as is manifestly obvious, the function of advertising is not solely promotion. In a truly free market information would also circulate in equal measure about the misinformation, incorrect assumptions and hidden dangers embedded in most forms of advertising. That is, a balanced field of information would address how to resist the sellers as well as how to be seduced by them. The psychology of consumer behaviour has never been concerned with resistance and has always sided, explicitly as well as implicitly, with those whose mission it is to sell goods irrespective of their moral or practical worth to individuals or society as a whole. Advertising's overriding purpose is to influence and persuade people to consume what they otherwise would not. Psychology has had an integral role in this since the early twentieth century. From the inception of psychoanalysis to the latest fads in 'neuro' speak[9] the behavioural sciences have played a prominent role in the big sell.

The Psychology of Marketing

Psychology's devotion to the current economic order is exemplified by the nature of its alliance with marketing. The psychological models constructed to explain human behaviour 'in the market place' contain little that is recognisably human. Outsiders to the discipline, as well as those students crossing the threshold into it, have long been confused by the failure of the discipline to identify, locate and study people within what they think is its allotted subject space i.e. the domain of personhood, existence and human relations. Just as psychology in general has replaced the notion of a person with the mirage of the genetically driven, biologically constituted, information-processing organism, so its offspring, 'consumer psychology,' has made the object of its study a 'consumer': a hypothetical 'entity' programmed to engage in information-processing and problem-solving about what to acquire and consume. "In the commercial world," Sparks writes, we are simply "automated all-consuming robots, not human beings" (2014, p.461). The complex world in which we live is similarly reduced to what retailers can control and manipulate. It is this manipulable context that is referred to as the retail or consumer environment. One might be forgiven for thinking that the point of all this is for companies to find or induce "someone to buy whatever the firm happens to manufacture," but no; according to Foxall, Goldsmith & Brown it is about "the satisfaction of consumer needs" (1998, p.3). The wording here is important – it is not the satisfaction of one's human needs which is at stake, but one's *consumer* needs.

Thus the fully fledged person is to be reconfigured as a consumer. And how is that done? It is achieved by conceptually eliminating the corpus of human needs one has and reimagining the totality of the human organism as a 'consumer.' The prevailing piecemeal psychology which compartmentalises the disciplinary subject matter of psychology into 'cognitive,' 'developmental,' 'biological,' 'personality' and 'social' domains is thus a ready-made conceptual aid for this project. What this process of re-imagination entails is that people's actual needs must first be invented (or massively distorted) before they can be realised and reinvented practically in the market place. The theoretical basis of marketing is, thus, from the outset disingenuous. The purpose of this elaborative reconstruction of the person as consumer is precisely to get an individual to buy whatever firms manufacture. The so-called values, aspirations, needs, desires and wants, even the 'personality' and 'identity' of the 'customer' must perforce be constructed and shaped by entrepreneurs, investors, designers, manufacturers, market researchers, psychologists and sellers. This is evident in the ubiquitous rise of the brand dissected by Klein in *No Logo*. For brand loyalty to take route and for people to erect a false and elevated sense of self-esteem centred on loyalty or attachment to the products they purchase and display (or merely talk about) presupposes not only a deep sense of alienation but also the prior existence of a sense of self which, before it can be reconstituted in business-friendly terms, must first be systematically undermined, threatened, subdued or demolished outright. Within the class-driven societies we inhabit, the never-ending promotion of celebrity and status is part of the plan of attack. We can then be invited or seduced to buy back what we lack. It was no accident that Marx's theoretical treatment of human life – a life shrunken and degraded through capitalist social relations – was nevertheless rooted in a firm humanistic perspective which encompassed other dreams and possibilities. These are possibilities unbeknown or imagined by brand psychologists and marketeers: the dreams of a better life, free from drudgery and open to the realisation of an un-alienated being.

Oblivious to the alienation at the heart of the brand phenomenon, psychologists have proposed a distinction between 'spurious' and 'true' brand loyalty, identifying the latter as possessing genuine commitment to the branded product (Bloemer and Kasper, 1995). In a consumer world predicated on falsity, what exactly 'genuine' is supposed to mean is probably best left to consumer philosophers. No doubt in the department store of ideas they can be found. With brand loyalty posited as some inherent facet of reality, the scientific quest for the marketing Holy Grail has been to identify what predicts it. The procedure involves the purchase (or not) of a given product being subject to the theoretical frameworks employed to understand human behaviour in other realms, notably in social and health psychology. These 'social cognition' models see a given behavioural act as the outcome of a series of prior, quantifiable, internal processes. The models derive their name from the fact that they envisage action in the social world arising from prior cognitive processes. However they have been heavily criticised (Ogden, 2003), not only because there are no agreed conventions on how to measure these hypothetical internal processes but also because they have been monumentally unsuccessful in predicting behaviour; all the more so when the behaviour of interest – usually drug use, sex, or alcohol use – unfolds in a dynamic social environment. Marketeers' interest in such models however is closely tied to their belief that the supermarket environment can be rigidly and tightly controlled and that the human behaviour exhibited within them is controllable and malleable: the aversion of Skinnerian and Pavlovian psychology with the adjunct of a supermarket trolley. This perspective of measurement and control has a long history in psychology, perhaps most infamously in B.F. Skinner's experiments in operant conditioning. In his wild and dark imagination Skinner envisaged the frightening vista of a fully behaviourally engineered society (see Skinner, 2002). Hence we must emphasise the fact that theoretical interest in human behaviour in the field of marketing is primed not on a desire to understand but a desire to control. In her critique of the social cognition approach, health psychologist Jane Ogden remarked that the models employed, rather than being value-neutral in what they purportedly observe and describe, in fact "create and change both cognitions and behaviour" and for that reason alone we must tread carefully (2003, p.427).

Schmitt (2012), somewhat unconsciously, provides a good summary of the current widespread malaise in 'brand' psychology. In drawing together the inter-relationships between the various psychological permutations on the brand – brand categorization, brand affect, brand personality, brand symbolism and brand attachment, "among others" – into a comprehensive framework rooted in "consumer-neuroscience" (p.7), what gets demonstrated yet again is not merely psychology's support for business but how it actively participates in interiorising the social, political and economic relations of late capitalism. When these structures work their way into the neural architecture of our brains, they can be reified and reinterpreted, firstly by the gullible scientists and secondly by the public, as natural material phenomena existing at the biological level. It is then a small step to project this imagined biology back out onto the world in order to explain it. Framing things in this way helps researchers to justify their career choices and actions, while the consequences for the public include the fatuous mystification of scientific truth as well as tragic distortion of the human possibilities open to them.

'Consumer neuroscience,' also described as 'neuromarketing' (Georges, Bayle-Tourtoulou & Badoc, 2013) and 'neuro-economics' (Dietz, 2011) has become the latest fad in marketing hype. Along with the religious worship of the brand the marketing devout have a professed faith in the notion of distinct personality types. It is no surprise then to see the marketing practice of categorising consumers – which was previously built around various hierarchies of social class – leap onto the neuroscience bandwagon. Natalie Nahai, the first self-proclaimed 'web-psychologist,' provides a telling example. Nahai advances the fatuous notion of neurochemical archetypes to simultaneously market not only herself but also the dubious notion that "our personalities are a product of our genes and neurochemicals" (2012, p.61). The vast literature on the situational determinants of behaviour and the role of other people, places, language and culture in making us who we are is apparently unable to attract her attention. But as I have tried to make clear in these pages, attention to the 'other' has never been a strong point in a psychology which has placed all attention on the individual. Nahai goes on to declare that human personality can be grouped into four temperamental styles (explorer, builder, negotiator and director[10]) governed by the prevalence of particular neurotransmitters in our brains, and that considered knowledge of these can help business men and women in developing a coherent marketing strategy. "Well, if you can ascertain what 'type' of personality your service or product is likely to attract," she writes, "you can design your website and user experience to specifically target and attract this type" (p.61). This is an instruction manual for selling snake oil!

Nahai claims her intentions are geared to the enhancement of human interaction with technology so that we can get our human needs met while businesses can "sell with integrity" (p.xiv). In reality she belongs to a business consortium which boasts of working "with some of the world's largest brands to change people's minds and behaviour for the better"[11]. Who decides what is for the best remains unsaid. As such she is one of a new generation of sales staff and her musings should be seen as little more than a sales pitch, possessing no more scientific credibility than astrology. Business though has always incorporated pseudo-science to boost sales. The oft repeated myth that we only ever use 10 per cent of our brain is a prime example. The claim received widespread attention in the 1970s when psychologist Georgi Lozanov repeated it as part of his efforts to promote his 'suggestopedia' method of language learning.

Integral to the grand scheme of consumer psychology and manipulating consumer behaviour is the careful orchestration of the social and physical environment. Micro-retail design is however not simply about facilitating people's 'shopping experience'[12] so that it is as painless, comfortable and carefree as can be. In fact the opposite is true. One needs only to be reminded of the continual reorganisation of supermarket shopping spaces – something which is in fact designed to disorient the person doing the shopping and to reorient them to spending more. Accustomed to finding particular products at specific locations, in the redesigned psycho-geographic environment of the hypermarket, the confused shopper will now wander haphazardly in search of the items they require, taking them past aisles containing arrays of previously unseen (and unwanted) products, set out to catch their eye and their money. The aim on the part of the supermarkets is to tempt people into buying products they had no intention of purchasing when they entered the shop. The manipulation of retail space to promote consumer spending may involve changes to a store's ambience as well as product placement and design, for example the type of lighting used (soft v bright), the tempo of the music played in the background or even the smell in the air. Lewis (2013) notes for example how casinos have even used scented aromas to relax gamers and slow the perceived passage of time. Added to this is the manipulation of shoppers' decision-making 'space' under the guise of choice architecture: the latest fad in behavioural economics.

Behavioural Economics: The Nudge

Behavioural economics has been described as a "serious academic discipline that can positively impact business"[13]. The leading edge of this, 'nudge' theory so-called, is ostensibly derived from the insights of Nobel Prize-winning psychologist Daniel Kahneman, whose work has highlighted a series of underlying biases in human cognition. Kahneman (2012) has argued that these biases are rooted in the operation and inter-action of two quite distinct systems of thinking: a rapid-response automatic system and a slower more reflective system. These lead people to adopt a number of simple rules of thumb in order to make decisions in an increasingly complex world. Kahneman's Nobel Prize was in fact awarded in economics, which itself says something about the relationship between the two disciplines and the kinds of decisions that people make which are of interest to policy makers, business leaders and ideologically unaware psychologists. In important respects economics as the study of rational choice (Chang, 2014) and cognitive psychology as the study of decision-making (incorporating learning, memory, thinking and perception) are merging into one rebranded as 'decision science.' An intellectual act of unconditional surrender on the part of the supposed science of the soul, one could very well argue!

Nudge theory enjoys support in high political places. As *The Guardian* reported, "a 'nudge unit' set up by David Cameron in the Cabinet Office is working on how to use behavioural economics and market signals to persuade citizens to behave in a more socially integrated way" (Wintour, 2010). The renamed 'Behavioural Insight Team' at the Prime Minister's service is advised by Richard Thaler, a leading proponent of nudge theory (see Thaler & Sunstein, 2009), to spearhead the idea that "governments can design environments that make it easier for people to choose what is best for themselves and society" (Wintour, 2010). Naturally enough these ideas are predicated on a number of unexamined assumptions.

First of all there is the implicit view, unquestioned by Thaler & Sunstein in their exposition of nudge theory, that it is not the capitalist system that requires change, nor the principle at its heart – of economic growth in a planet with finite resources – nor the nature of increasingly undemocratic government. Instead, their avowed focus is on the conditions under which individuals make choices to supposedly enhance their health, wealth and happiness. Therein lays the second problematic assumption: that it is the well-being of individuals and not collectives that is at stake. The serious limitations of this are evident throughout Thaler and Sunstein's exposition. For example they acknowledge that "greed and corruption helped to create the (financial) crisis" (Thaler & Suntein, p.260), but rather than acknowledge that the system they support is actually premised on these characteristics and that their consequences have effected people *en masse*, they instead divert attention to the role of individual "human frailty" (p.79) resulting from the effects of 'bounded rationality,' (where people are unable to arrive at optimal solutions to problems due to insufficient cognitive resources, unfamiliarity with a problem and the absence of feedback) as well as lack of "self-control" and the effects of "social influences."

The contradiction between setting up as targets for change, the consequences of decisions which result from individual human frailties, and the acknowledgement that companies have a "strong incentive to cater to (and profit from) human frailties" goes unexamined (p.79). If governments are to be the primary agents behind the enactment of large-scale nudges designed to alter human behaviour then there is absolutely no possibility that they can be trusted to do so in a manner which truly benefits the citizens they govern. This will remain the case so long as the same agents of big business, which not only profit from human frailty but actively promote it, move in and out of government with disconcerting regularity – a phenomena described by Morgan as "a revolving door through which ex-politicians glide effortlessly into the capitalist utopia" (2014, p.21). Such is the extent of this that government itself now functions largely as just another tier in the management of business interests: a major factor in the declining confidence which people (internationally) have in the legitimacy of their political elites and the disconcerting re-emergence of ethnic politics on the European stage. The conflict of interest between worker/citizen and organs of big business which formed the basis of Marx's analysis is nowhere here acknowledged let alone addressed.

At best Thaler and Sunstein's discussion of nudge theory can be said to be naïve; at worst, it is positively dangerous – a tool for widespread social and behavioural engineering in the hands of powerful political and business elites. Dietz (2011) contrasts Thaler and Sunstein's naïve optimism regarding professional persuaders with Robert Cialdini's (2006) more measured concerns. Using much the same scientific literature, Cialdini's stance is scathing of the 'compliance professionals' behind sales and marketing campaigns. Psychologists, unsurprisingly, constitute a sizeable proportion of these professional groups who seek to manipulate us in directions which are not in our best interests. The political interest in these ideas is, naturally, to produce a mass psychology conducive to the interests of the powerful. The "fateful marriage" between "mass psychology and schemes of corporate and political persuasion" (cited in Lewis, 2013, p.13) is not in itself new, but as part of the post-war landscape of political-economy it should be considered a danger to democracy. The danger is all the greater when the people subject to this engineering are not even aware of it. The historical record, suffice to say, gives no grounds for comfort. The ethical problems associated with nudge theory do not end with the assumptions which it embodies. A consideration of some of the principal areas considered ripe for intervention makes this plain.

To illustrate the potential utility of nudge theory, Thaler and Sunstein explore the potential benefits of applying large-scale nudges in the areas of savings, investments, the operation of credit markets and the privatisation of social security. To be fair to them, they are often critical of the manner in which policies and practices in these areas have been developed. However in anchoring their prime examples in the field of finance they are seemingly unaware that what they are in fact proposing is a means to make money markets more efficient – not just to the humble citizen, but to institutions and institutional investors. Thaler's insistence that government adopt longer term horizons is hopelessly naïve about the tripartite relationship between government, citizens and big business. No doubt some longer-term thinking – notably around environmental sustainability and the use of natural resources – is overdue and desperately needed. Yet Thaler, typical of those who advance solutions to political problems on the basis of the behaviour of individual actors, seems to lack any real understanding of how, by its very nature, the capitalist economic system is predicated on short-term gain and how any attempts to challenge this necessarily generate conflict.

The UK welfare capitalism of the post-war period, as well as the more socially oriented variants in Germany and Japan, have all fallen by the wayside in the face of the ruthless neo-liberal Anglo-American juggernaut. Anything which stands in the way of short-term profit is now simply brushed aside. Without the threat posed by the existence of the Soviet Union and its allies, there is insufficient leverage to force any concessions from the capitalist elite, especially as the system concentrates ever greater levels of wealth in their hands. The level of support globally for communist and socialist reforms threatened immediate short-term profits. That climate change and destruction of the biosphere – considered as events which unfold over decades if not centuries – do not, tells us much about why business continues in its customary fashion. The science of the 'nudge' finds favour at the current time precisely because it does not call for wholesale structural reform of the economic system. Nudge theory is concerned with advocating particular forms of corporate and government action to shape mass psychology within a climate of minimal regulation. Little wonder it has attracted business interest and support. As the zone of responsibility and decision-making in the theory is focused on individuals, little wonder that psychologists are at the heart of it. As economist Ha-Joon Chang (2014) has observed, economic theory is always linked to political purpose; there is no value-free neutral science to be found in it. At the end of the day nudge theory is premised on maintaining the status quo of a consumer society. Promising enhanced well-being to individuals through benign corporate-engineered architectures of choice, it is not so much self-help for individuals which is on offer as a message of 'help yourself' to those who run big business.

Business Psychology

Marketing and behavioural economics are both geared toward changing consumer behaviour. However the consumer is but one side of the behavioural equation. Persistence of the ethos, management and organisation of the business status quo depends in large measure on the actions of those who most profit from propping up the systems of exploitation. Robert Cialdini described the conduct of the requisite professional elite behind this as inherently treacherous toward consumers, exploiting deeply felt human responses (for example reciprocity, liking, commitment, consistency and authority) in order to maximise gain (Cialdini & Cliffe, 2013). The elite comprises a steady supply of business leaders, managers, sales and marketing personnel, not to mention professional psychologists, all of whom are required to ensure the system runs smoothly. They are aided in this quest by the emerging field of business psychology.

The Association for Business Psychology describes business psychology as "the study and practice of improving working life. It combines an understanding of the science of human behaviour with experience of the world of work to attain effective and sustainable performance for both individuals and organisations"[14]. Whilst the first part of this definition is congruent with the aims of the Trades Union movement, one would be hard pressed to find any explicit mention on the ABP's website of the interests of working people and how these might flourish in a business environment. Instead we are informed that the ABP is committed to an approach which is "practical" and "business-led." This business-led approach prioritises management needs and is focused on a number of key areas: selection and assessment (including psychometric testing), organisational development, leadership development, employee engagement, performance management and appraisal, work culture and health and well-being at work. These could all be legitimate concerns of employee organisations and as areas of interest are in many ways quite laudable; the problems arise when one considers what the larger organisational aims actually are and the nature of the ethical, legal and political contexts in which they are embedded.

With respect to the broader business environment, Bakan's 2005 critique of "The Corporation" is instructive. In the current globalised climate, corporations function de facto as legally constituted psychopaths, empowered and structured to pursue self-interest above all else. If the asymmetry in power and fundamental conflict of interest between the organisation and its employees is not recognised or acknowledged then any subsequent interventions by psychologists, business or otherwise, will do little or nothing to address what is fundamentally wrong. If we look a little closer behind the key areas of interest for business psychologists, one could legitimately ask for example what exactly 'employee engagement' means other than the co-option and engagement of the workforce with the aims and aspirations of management. Are business psychologists going to promote union leadership or forms of resilience in the workforce to defend working people's interests? Let's take as a further illustrative example a recent report by the Chartered Institute for Personnel and Development (CIPD, 2012), the professional body for human resource staff. The authors of this report acknowledge that in the wake of the financial crash and the bank bail-outs, public confidence has been "profoundly destabilised... resulting in a breakdown in trust in government and business" (p.3). They go on to say that "understanding how to maintain and not lose trust in the first place becomes a key management contributor to better business performance" (p.3). This looks like a plea for workers to maintain faith in a system which manifestly does not warrant it. Furthermore, as the authors argue that organisational trust is strongly influenced by the twin factors of line managers' behaviour and of employees feeling trusted by management, one is left to ponder how the accelerating surveillance at the workplace (and outside it) – designed to maximise profit – is going to enhance trust. The impression given is that management belief in workplace trust is a lot like the British Government's championing of democracy in its foreign policy. If their policy aims are supported by local democratic regimes, all is well and good for public image; but if not then the aims take precedence anyway and the ideals of democracy are given short shrift. In a nutshell, democracy and workplace trust are expendable. The goals – as ever with business and organisational psychologists – are to repair the current dysfunctional system or otherwise prop it up. As with behavioural economics a dynamic maintenance of the status quo is the assumed default option over radical change. One is reminded of Gogol's lament, at the end of one of his short stories. It is an apt conclusion for the emancipatory potential of business and consumer psychology: "monotonous rain and a tearful sky without one ray of sunlight... It's a dreary world, gentlemen!" (2005, p.77).

Chapter 6

Psychology and Capitalism

What makes us capable of changing our minds and questioning our world views?
(Boym, 2010, p.256)

I thought I discerned the basis of a historically concrete and revolutionary psychology in which the real life of the individual is understood as the interiorisation of political relations.
(Sève, 1978, p.2)

In this book a radical basis for understanding the nature of the discipline of psychology has been set out. The critique is in effect a discussion of the political economy of psychology, and proposes a number of avenues through which it contributes to the forward march of capitalism. That psychology has been a bedfellow of capitalism is a serious proposition, yet it is one that many people in the field who profess an interest in human well-being seem scarcely to have considered. One has to find this alarming. One does not need to be a Marxist to concur with Marx's position that "awareness of reality as a key to change is... one of the conditions of social progress" (Fromm, 1973, p.83). Psychology seems to have a blind faith that it can contribute to social progress while remaining oblivious and downright hostile to acknowledging connections to anything remotely political. This is the avowed stance of the British Psychological Society, a position it defends on the grounds of its charitable status. For a good many psychologists the well-being of the people they imagine they are providing a service for is not associated with the general political economy or socio-economic foundations of society. This is a position which even empirically is indefensible.

One might just as well consider any form of psychology which persists in such denial as embracing the "future of an illusion" to borrow a phrase from Freud (2008).

Under its current structure and modus operandi, and contrary to the picture given by the huge amount of publicity it generates, psychology has not advanced theoretical understanding of the human condition. That is it has not produced a viable interpretative framework which fully incorporates either our behavioural contributions (individual and social) to the world or our experience in it. Neither has it provided a viable body of knowledge for lay people to utilise constructively in order to understand either the nature of their subjective experiential states, or the nature of the major influences on human action in the world. What it has managed to do is promote itself as a science of de-contextualised, de-historicised, alienated individuals who are to be understood not as persons but as purely material objects in a universe subject to cause and effect relationships which can be manipulated and controlled according to the contingent interests of wider (untheorised) political and economic interests. How it has managed to do this is summarised in a series of statements below.

1) Psychology appropriates human characteristics which are at least partly social and transfers these, both theoretically and practically, into the individual realm.

In an earlier chapter it was discussed how psychology responds to the capitalist system by reifying the logic of industrial production in terms of a hypothetical set of interiorised states, faculties or propensities which are then considered as the properties of individual people. The differences between people with respect to these concepts are then interpreted not in terms of people's differing life experiences but as reflective of essential differences (see no.2 below).

If we examine some of these psychological concepts a little

closer however another picture emerges. As these ideas now function in the broader knowledge economy they come to have the properties of commodities and have commercial value and utility for businesses. As the commodification of higher education continues alongside the de facto privatisation of the social sciences in the UK, the corporate influence upon the range of teaching and research conducted in psychology has never been greater. In line with this the discipline is more and more 'business friendly.' In this doubly 'privatised' form, psychological knowledge has, in common with Marx's (1990) general theory of commodities, functioned to conceal social relations. It has done this in at least two ways. Firstly in transferring the characteristics of social networks and social groupings entirely to the realm of individuals, psychological ideas sweep away the reality of the social and bolster an individualised view of reality. Secondly presenting such knowledge as claimed scientific truths then obscures the ideological function of the former process of individual 'acquisition' and presents the claimed ideas as nuggets of pure truth. Let us examine the first of these in greater detail.

Intelligence, memory, resilience, efficacy, attitudes and personality, all of which psychology has designated as aspects of individual functioning, in fact also exist to a significant degree in the social domain. The capitalist domination of science for example has promulgated a view of science as the work of lone geniuses. Nothing could be further from the truth. Science is always an intrinsically social activity, in which scientific products are always the outcome of a collective work of intelligence involving numerous contributors, each of whom adds something of value to the finished work. Thinking always proceeds more rapidly and effectively in a social context where others can listen as well as offer thoughts, ideas and suggestions. All of this moves the group toward the production of something which improves upon the capacity of any one individual.

Similarly the collective work of organised resistance to oppression can also be seen as a work of collective intelligence. The scientific, technological, legal, political and moral fruits of human productivity through the ages are also all works of collective intelligence.

Closely related to the social meaning of intelligence, resistance and resilience toward hardship can also be contemplated as existing not solely in an individual capacity but also as properties of social networks and communities. Psychology has recognised the importance of social ties and relationships in well-being, but has reduced these to the concept of social support which is considered a measurable resource possessed by individuals. This naturally enough leads to a very different conceptualisation of how existing affairs can be improved. Rather than attempting to facilitate the capacity to form greater friendships and ties in a given individual, the object of intervention might just as well be a given community, work or social group or indeed any oppressed group faced with the challenge of building collective resistance to life's hardships. As a result the entire notion of protest as a form of community resource is absent from psychological formulations of resilience. Efficacy likewise is about the capacity to wilfully engage in effective collective action in pursuit of both individual and group goals. One doesn't need to think far as to why an emphasis on such organised and collective empowerment has found little place in psychology. It is of interest that the work of Haslam & Reicher (2012), perhaps best known for their contribution to the BBC program *The Experiment* in which a modern-day variant of the Stanford Prison Experiment was conducted[16], have proposed working toward a social psychology of resistance. They note the default option in social psychology has all too often been to preclude "the possibility of resistance" and to "put the topic beyond the realm of scientific imagination" (p.154). Their work, unusually political for the discipline, is unfortunately unlikely to exert much influence across it given the fragmented nature of psychological thought. However the conceptual landscape mapped out by Haslam and Reicher exhibits a number of striking similarities with the suggestions which Tim Gee advanced in *Counterpower: Making Change Happen* (2011). Together they suggest possibilities for a very different kind of practical knowledge – one of how to successfully challenge established power – to be developed both inside and outside the discipline.

If we consider attitudes, which conventional psychology holds to be measurable relatively stable dispositions which exist in an individual toward another person, event, activity, object or idea, we are immediately faced with innumerable problems. These can be best illustrated by reference to the supposed phenomenon of stereotypes – though what follows could equally apply to the myriad superstitions, beliefs and ideologies held by millions. A stereotypical attitude can only properly be said to exist in a person if a good many other people also exhibit it. This leads to the question as to why a collection of people should all hold the same attitudinal set and at more or less the same time. One could presuppose that the requisite explanation is different for every individual; but that merely begs the question as to what mysterious social process produces more or less the same outcome throughout the society or community in which the stereotypical thought is manifest and hence it directs attention to the social origin of the phenomenon.

The solution to this conundrum is simple; and that is to regard attitudes not as pre-existing neurocognitive structures residing in the brain, awaiting expression only when a suitable social cue arrives, but as indicative of a wider set of socially distributed representations which constitute the 'organising agents' of individual thought. Thus when we think, we must do so making use of the only tools we have available: the ideas, notions and images which circulate throughout the society. Thus our social attitudes, not to say much of our general thought, can be considered as essentially social processes. This is the suggestion of the French social psychologist Serge Moscovici. In Moscovici's view, such social representations form the basis for a psychology of common sense as well as functioning as a unifying principle for all the social sciences (see Moscovici & Duveen, 2000). Moscovici maintained that social psychology in its contemporary incarnation was insufficiently critical to be a true science; it was imbued with a fetish for data and an obsession to conform to an outdated view of what passed for science. To truly be scientific, he argued, it must also become dangerous, willing to upset convention, and willing to embrace criticism as a political weapon. Needless to say, Moscovici remains on the margins of psychology where he and others who subscribe to his theory of social representations are dismissed as unscientific. Dangerous they no doubt are.

Closely related to attitudes is the thorny problem of personality, which psychology has erected as some ahistorical biologically based form of individuality – a view with little evidence to commend it. The various possibilities which exist at any one moment for the expression of character are of course limited by the broader set of existing economic and productive relations to say nothing of the socio-cultural mores of the groups to which one belongs. While postmodern theorists have pronounced the death of the author and reconfigured notions of the self as a developing assembly of social relations, mainstream psychology has remained fixated on a mathematically based approach to the analysis of personality based on linguistic descriptions of character. This assumes some mysterious hidden essence can explain the observable correlations between different personality descriptors. Thus far the psychology of personality has provided us with more information about the social and linguistic customs we employ to represent (i.e. describe) character than anything about the regularities people actually exhibit in their behaviour in the world and how these regularities may vary with time and place and even constitute part of what is referred to as the zeitgeist. For example the last twenty to thirty years have seen the rise of new forms of technology (computers, mobile technology and social media for example), in addition to patterns of work which have increasingly isolated people from established physical social spaces. There has in addition been considerable growth in personal advertising and marketing. Accompanying these productive changes has been a trend for increasing attention to be given to the self, corresponding to an escalating narcissism in the population. These developments in the expression of character clearly follow changes in the broader political economy and are closely tied not only to the level of industrial and technological development but also to design. It is no accident that the information revolution rode into town onto the backs of *personal* computers. Experimental psychology remains incapable of accounting for the social, political, and economic dimensions to character structure, something which psychoanalysis for all its sins has at least attempted on more than one occasion. Personality as such becomes just one more item on the growing list of psychological commodities produced under capitalism and one which appeals to the management consultancy and recruitment industry.

2) Psychology perpetuates alienation

As discussed in Chapter 3, psychology as a discipline takes our current alienated state as if it were a natural and unquestionable phenomenon. Two assumptions which the discipline makes contribute to this in large part. The first is to view human beings as if they were nothing but complex material objects existing 'out there,' rather than seeing ourselves as embodied active agents, who are responsible for our own actions and whose freedom and potential freedom always posits us as existing beyond the immediately given. Marx of course took the latter view, envisaging humanity as realising itself socially through historical action. Sartre too considered human life an ongoing project that, individually at least, only finished with our death. George Kelly's personal construct theory is also in principal historic, for it too depicts human beings as perpetually venturing into the unknown, that the truth of our lives lies perpetually "somewhere over the horizon" (1970, p.19). Kelly was acutely aware that psychological theories express values, that they implicitly adopt a particular stance toward people. The principle argument advanced in these pages is that the values which are implicitly endorsed in mainstream psychological theory and practice are those which form the mainstay of capitalist philosophy, ideology and practice.

The second assumption hard-wired into psychology provides an unending source of alienation. It is that our behaviour is explicable (again from an outsider perspective) as some combination of genetic and environmental influences. This sterile perspective has animated most branches of the discipline for some considerable time and through it has rendered it nigh on impossible for students of the discipline (and I include academic staff here as well) to maintain a professional view on the world which confers on themselves the ability to determine their own life and destiny. If they do manage to hold on to this possibility for themselves their personal lives remain split from the object of their academic concerns. At best then, if self-alienation is kept in check through denial of the relevance of one's professional concerns to oneself, then it will almost certainly be applied to others contributing to alienation from them. Within this nature-nurture dichotomy human affairs are reduced to the outcome of a ping-pong match between internal and external forces. Another possibility of course exists, and this again concerns the historical element.

Ironically, increased awareness of the historical dimension to human life has come about through the collapse of the communist system in Eastern Europe. This has led, in the social sciences beyond psychology, to serious engagement with issues concerning how the past is recalled, recollected and conveyed in different memory communities, as well as how the past is transmitted across generations within a given community. The breakdown of the Iron Curtain and the consequent migration of people from the former Soviet Bloc into Western Europe entails that the travelling populations have brought their individual and collective memories with them – narrative accounts of past events which in some instances differ markedly from the accounts Westerners have been brought up on. Not only has work on social memory revealed it to be as selective and biased as individual memory, but like individual memory it is linked to projects concerned with the maintenance of specific ideals and (social) identities. Social memory has thus been revealed to be subject to the same kinds of motivated remembering and forgetting which Freud noted as facets of individual memory. The work on social memory has added import not only because it chimes with Marx's claim that "the tradition of all dead generations weighs like a nightmare upon the brain of the living" (1852/2006, p.15) but because it points to a means by which the past might exert an influence outside of the realm of genetics or immediate environment. The influences on contemporary human behaviour are thus vertical as well as horizontal. Such a perspective not only casts new light on the dynamics occurring at any level of the social hierarchy – from families, through workplaces to the international political arena – it also offers a direct challenge to the dominant biological encrusted formulations of mental health and illness.

3) Psychology promotes mental health system oppression

Psychology, together with psychiatry and allied professions – what have come to be called the 'psy' professions – have contributed to the development of what has in some quarters been called mental health system oppression. This has two main components. First of all when human behaviour becomes problematic in any context it has become customary to try and identify defects within a given individual. In the absence of satisfactory evidence psychology has speculated that the problems are manifested in an individual person through biochemical or genetic defects they either possess or have inherited. Outside of more enlightened schools of thought – e.g. those connected with family therapy – for over 40 years it has been considered virtually taboo to consider such problems as arising from structural violence, dysfunctional social dynamics, or patterns of disturbed interpersonal communication between people. In addition the emphasis on biology has meant that more obvious explanations of psychological difficulties, for example mistreatment by other people, have been neglected. The kind of 'vulgar' psychology that this gives rise to, creates the basis for victim-blaming.

Secondly, with the mental health system predicated on this notion of 'defective individuals,' the dissemination of this model throughout society has given rise to a widespread pattern in both the public and the private sphere whereby disagreements between people, even of a relatively mild nature, result in derogatory attributions being made about the supposed mental health of those with whom one disagrees[15]. As Szasz suggests, the incursion of psychiatric and psychological thinking into political discourse has by now become so routine that the list of the accused has become virtually "endless" (1983, p.120). As such, the linguistic-psychological abuse – by means of attributions of mental instability – of those who challenge or upset power at any level, be it in any organisation, is now so thoroughly ingrained in the mind-set of the powerful that it gives all the appearance of being a reflex action. This contributes not only to the insidious medicalisation of everyday life but also to the psychologisation of politics and with it the mystification of political interest and power. This can see events such as the invasion of Iraq and the use of military power to enforce corporate interests in energy resources reduced to absurd pronouncements about the supposed mental health of George Bush or Tony Blair just because they were the ultimate political authorities sanctioning the war. This is turn reinforces the everyday working of the mental health system where notions of illness are considered primary explanations of people's conduct rather than the interests, reasons or motives behind it being sought.

4) Psychology promotes surveillance, militarism and social control

One consequence of the increasing privatisation of stress (Fisher, 2009) – aided and abetted by psychological concepts of individual deficiency in the midst of deteriorating social conditions – is that people come to look increasingly at themselves as the source of their difficulties. Advertising adds to stress by continually providing unrealistic role models and impossible standards with respect to both physical and psychological well-being. In response to this people regularly inspect themselves for any indication of imperfection. This self-surveillance is mirrored by psychology's specific contribution, via work on face recognition, to the widespread public surveillance characteristic of the security state. These developments, which have proceeded without any firm democratic controls, pose serious threats to civil liberties. The intention behind them is to enable the authorities to identify and track people 'of interest,' who often will be people engaged in exercising their legitimate democratic rights to protest and organise. As the crisis of capitalism deepens and the attempts to shore up the existing order become more desperate, it is likely that this technology, which is still in its infancy, will play an increasing part in social control.

Psychology's contributions to social control do not end there. The mental health system's function of pathologising human difference and its role in spreading fear of others helps create the licence for state-sanctioned intervention, against people's expressed wishes, to control their behaviour and render it more manageable to the authorities. It has also allowed states the world over to regard people's undesired political behaviour as signs of mental disorder. It is no accident that statistics point to members of oppressed groups – working-class people, ethnic minorities, women, gay people and disabled people – as being not only foremost amongst the psychiatric/psychological casualties of the current order, but also more likely to be subject to coercive, demeaning and degrading physical interventions (electric shock treatment, forced drugging, brain surgery) in order to render their behaviour more compliant. It is certainly ironic that one widely accepted definition of terrorism – the use or threatened use of force against civilian populations for political purposes (Patel, 2007, p.75) – applies equally well to the operation of the mental health system. Using the maxim that members of the 'psy' professions be defined on the basis of what they actually *do* rather than what they say they do, the above definition of terrorism begins to read like a job description. Simply put, the 'psy' professions use or threaten to use ECT, drugs, 'psychosurgery' or involuntary hospitalisation against people for political purposes i.e. social control, protection of embarrassed governing elites or regimes and enhancement of their own political and professional power. It is a measure of the mental health system's success in dispensing propaganda that this proposition may at first seem outlandish. However it is readily apparent in the numerous accounts relayed by psychiatric survivors (e.g. Read & Reynolds, 2000) and warrants more widespread discussion.

In addition to the above, behavioural science opens up several other avenues of social control. The largest of these, at least in terms of the magnitude of the effects produced (as well as the number of psychologists employed to assist in bringing these effects about) is the military. As Richards (2002) notes the considerable financing of psychological work by the defence industries remains hidden from view. Direct psychological assistance to the military has a long history, dating back at least to the First World War. The principal aims of this have been to change and shape the values, ideas, emotions, reasoning and behaviour of the target audience, who are as likely to be the domestic population as they are the civilian population of the supposed enemy. A very thin line exists between this and all-out propaganda. Hitler's appointment of Joseph Goebbels as Propaganda Minister owed much to his view that a decisive factor in Germany losing the First World War had been the psychological tactics employed by the British. Not surprisingly research on mass communication, persuasion and attitude change has occupied a significant place in the psychology curriculum for some time. The modern public relations industry owes much to this. Freud's nephew, Edward Bernays, is considered its 'father.' Bernays, drawing on propaganda, crowd psychology and psychoanalysis, was clear that the industry he sponsored was one which was intent on mass deceit. He called it "engineering consent" (1955, p.8). He proffered the view that Goebbels had given propaganda a bad name, hence it was in need of a new one. That *Life* magazine voted him one of the 100 most influential Americans of the 20th century is a measure of his success in orchestrating mass deception on behalf of corporate America.

Amongst the noted psychologists to have taken money from the defence industry purse is the famous humanist psychotherapist Carl Rogers, who received funding from the CIA front organisation, the Society for the Investigation of Human Ecology. The CIA's interests lay in mind control and mind manipulation (see Chapter 4). Rogers made his own ignoble contribution to this cause in order to participate in the fight against the 'menace' of communism. "It's impossible to realize what it was like in the 1950s," said Rogers (cited in Harper, 2007, p.19). This is the same Rogers who wrote, "I feel a deep concern that the developing behavioural sciences may be used to control the individual and rob him of his personhood" (1961, foreword). Maybe it is not possible to know what it was truly like in the 1950s. And no doubt for those legions of psychologists currently aiding the military-industrial complex it will later prove impossible to realise what it was like in the 2010s. Stanley Milgram's famous shock experiments are also rumoured to have been funded by the US government.

In the military armoury, courtesy of psychology, last but by no means least, is the use of torture and 'enhanced' interrogation techniques. As is acknowledged within the psychological community, though not often and not very loudly, psychologists working for government agencies have refined these techniques to ensure they produce complete mental breakdown. The principal techniques (see Chapter 4) now in use were largely developed in the course of sensory deprivation research carried out in the 1960s. Participation in military interrogations (read: torture) has actually been forbidden by both the American Psychiatric Association and the American Medical Association. The American Psychological Association, no doubt mindful of the role of the US military in bankrolling much psychological research, has refused to outlaw participation of its members in such activities. The British Psychological Society, while not explicitly endorsing it, largely turns a blind eye to it, through its ever-ready mantra of not wishing to get involved in anything political.

The most recent addition to the tools which psychology has provided for maintaining the capitalist status quo goes by the name of behavioural economics. This has emerged from cognitive psychologists' interests in decision-making under conditions of risk and uncertainty as well as developments in evolutionary psychology and game theory. Theorists hope to offer improved predictability of the behaviour of players in the financial markets, naturally enough to enable them to make more money more efficiently. There is the additional boon that psychologists' efforts here can shore up the classical economic models which notably failed to predict the financial crisis of 2007. Psychology has also joined forces with economics under the guise of nudge theory to investigate subtle means of producing behavioural change at the population level. Politicians have not been slow to realise the latent possibilities for shifting population behaviour toward favoured policy goals. The idea is to alter mass behaviour in a predictable way without significantly changing people's economic incentives. From the desired policy angle in the White House or Downing Street, this entails compliance with the capitalist consumer agenda while claiming people can be 'nudged' toward greater well-being and happiness as the planetary ecosystem implodes under the weight of capitalist exploitation.

5) Psychology depoliticises social space

The worst of the 'sins' contained in the discipline of psychology is not just that it creates and celebrates a limiting and alienating vision of humanity which serves the needs and wants of a global psychopathic financial system, but that it acts to create not merely the vision but also the actuality of alienated being. It can only have had the success it has enjoyed so far in doing so, by being able to cover its tracks. As scientific psychology seeks to erase the historical space from accounts of human conduct and experience it simultaneously seeks to erase and rewrite its own history. Of all the academic disciplines psychology is perhaps the most adept in the "art of enforced amnesia" (Boym, 2010, p.9). Perhaps the biggest lie in this wholesale revision of the past (and the present) is that psychology produces objective knowledge that is apolitical and free from political influence. It purports to stand outside and above from all political disputes and conflicts of interest and justice. Miraculously, while claiming to do this it freely circulates the ambition that it alone beats a path to the end of human suffering, the greatest of which is caused by the very injustices, abuses and inequalities in power which it steadfastly refuses to engage with. The undesirable truth for those whose place is at the heart of the profession is that this position is untenable. The 'view from nowhere' which scientists of all persuasions profess to seek is in fact always a view from somewhere. Truth is always to be found from specific vantage points not impossible ones. That there could be such a thing as an 'objective' stance rooted in an emotionless, pain-free zone of rationality, forever beyond the clutches of the misery and uncertainty of this time and this place, is a fiction – an aberrant obsession. It is best to be honest about it, rather than doubling one's efforts to hide it. Presented as an attempt to reveal reality, psychology is in fact an organised, increasingly corporate-funded project to escape from the conditioned, socio-political historical nature of it.

Psychological discourse chiefly inhabits a space which ought to be occupied by political and moral debate. The problems between us do not originate within us, even if the effects may sometimes come to be felt there. The desire, and the search, for a just world cannot be replaced by a technical fix. Just as one cannot make a silk purse from a sow's ear, one cannot conjure, least of all through social engineering, a 'good' world from an imagined value-free neutral zone. This we must endeavour to create in the only way in which it might be possible: through the trial and error of messy, contingent human action.

Psychologists have a critical decision to make and they do not have very long to think about it. In the Communist Party Manifesto, Marx famously declared that the capitalist mode of production sweeps away "all fixed fast-frozen relations," that, "all that is solid melts into air" (1975, pp.36-7). Psychology too may meet this fate. As a unified discipline it increasingly faces stern competition from its own intellectual offspring; a victim of its own capitalist success, it is to be swept from view by the expanding market of neuroscience. The irony of this and the resonance of its potential demise with the myth of King Oedipus may sadly be lost on many in the discipline. As traditional academic values are swept away by the capitalist tsunami and intellectual endeavour of all kinds becomes subordinated to the calculus of profit and loss, where then do we stand in the desire to create a better world? The situation is critical.

Academics have always been marked by a "conformist subservience to those in power" (Chomsky, 2004, p.48) so we should not be too optimistic that psychology can avoid drifting into a totalitarian ideology. However it remains true that as Chomsky (1967) noted during the Vietnam War; "intellectuals are in a position to expose the lies of governments, to analyze actions according to their causes and motives and often hidden intentions". In his account of his obedience studies Milgram wrote that "obedience is the psychological mechanism that links individual action to political purpose" (1974, p.19). So too, psychology's obedience to capitalist imperatives links it to political purpose. A significant number of participants in those studies refused to obey the experimenter exhorting them to shock one of their fellows. It is incumbent upon those who call themselves psychologists, as well as those who study the subject, to resist psychology's implicit political purposes. This resistance needs to encompass not merely the discipline's manifest rightward political embrace but also the forms of subjectivity which this imposes upon us all.

This is a challenging task. Marx called for the "reform of consciousness not by dogmas but by the analysis of the mythical consciousness unclear to itself" (cited in Fromm, 1973, p.83). The mythical mind-set of the present unbeknownst to many is shaped by contemporary psychology to a remarkable degree. In the present moment there is a pressing need to dissect and perhaps discard it. Whether an emancipatory psychology can be salvaged from its enduring bourgeois enslavement is an unknown – a matter for our future deliberation and action. At the very least this would require that we interrogate both psychology and our visions of emancipation. In both these tasks we must strive to de-centre our current experience and move off-world from the corporate-imperial psychologised consciousness which both saturates and impedes our imagined possibilities. Psychology in many ways is a fairy tale, a part of modern folklore promising the 'magic' of technically engineered happy endings. It is my conjecture that the world will appear a different and more promising place without it. We must rethink the place of the subjective within the matrix of the social, cultural, historical and political. We must seek to link the psychological to the political not through obedience as Milgram observed but through enlisting the more noble human possibilities: of love, mutual care, inspiration, imagination, the management and elimination of fear and the artistic creation of alternative ways of seeing and being.

The picture painted in this book is not a rosy one. However our resistance to the state of affairs depicted in it must be crafted with due respect to the uncertainties of life and an honest and open acknowledgement that right now we *really* do not know what to do. To take up residence in the unknown may yet prove to be the safer and wiser option. Utopian and dangerous dreams have perennially shadowed the worlds brought into being by those with faith in certitude and unbending trust in both destiny and their own authority. Facts are never what they seem – least of all psychological ones. Better hope than a cast-iron 'truth' which is the enemy of possibility. But there *is* always resistance, and because of it, an ineradicable core of freedom, and with it dignity, remains at the heart of the human condition. Only from resistance is the "infinite improbability"[17] of a better world possible.

Endnotes

1. A term used by Dimitrijevic (2011) to describe a state engaging in mass crime supported from its civilian base.
2. In an article published in 2007, a group of authors noted that trying to get work published that described behaviour without inferring such 'internal processes' was "more trouble than it is worth" (Baumeister, Vohs & Funder, p.401).
3. The philosopher Paul Tillich described existentialism as "an over one hundred year old movement against the dehumanization of man in industrial society" (see Fromm, 2011, p.46).
4. A group which, though constituted as a single group by the socio-economic system, is comprised of members who behave toward one another as if they had no common interest.
5. See http://en.wikipedia.org/wiki/War_Is_a_Racket (Accessed March 2014).
6. See http://en.wikipedia.org/wiki/Political_psychology (Accessed March 2014).
7. See http://www.youtube.com/watch?v=hN_-HTjy-_w. (Accessed June 2014).
8. Interestingly, variations in the desire to arrange one's life by credit card have not been subject to behavioural genetic analysis. At least not yet; perhaps the perils of gene theory will put right what nature got wrong.
9. The resemblance between this and Orwell's newspeak is not merely phonetic; its use is intended to change what you think and how you think about it.
10. Nahai acknowledges anthropologist Helen Fisher as the source of this idea.
11. See http://www.ogilvychange.com/ (Accessed June 2014).
12. Note how from higher education, through adventure holidays to shopping, capitalism has moved on to selling us experience.

13. See http://www.ogilvychange.com/ for this assault on grammar. (Accessed May 2014).
14. See http://www.theabp.org.uk/about/what-is-business-psych ology.aspx (Accessed June 2014).
15. The original Stanford Prison Experiment, conducted by Philip Zimbardo and funded by the US Office of Naval Research, examined what happened when a group of volunteers were arbitrarily assigned to the roles of either prisoners or guards in a simulated prison environment. Due to the authoritarian and unpleasant nature of the guards' behaviour during the study, the experiment was brought to a premature end.
16. See for example David Owen's (2008) attributions of mental illness to Tony Blair and John F. Kennedy.
17. See Boym (2010) for an extended discussion, following Arendt, of freedom as the miracle of the 'infinitely improbable.' A reality which though infinitely improbable, occurs regularly and publically.

References

American Psychiatric Association (APA). (1987) *Diagnostic and Statistical Manual of Mental Disorders* (3rd edition, revised). (DSM-III-R). Washington: APA.

Bakan, J. (2005) *The Corporation: The Pathological Pursuit of Profit and Power*. London: Constable.

Bannister, D. & F. Fransella. (1971) *Inquiring Man*. Harmondsworth: Penguin.

Banyard, P. (2004). "Terrorism asking the right questions." Letters. *The Psychologist*, 17 (11): p.624.

Baumeister, R.F., K.D. Vohs & D.C. Funder. (2007) "Psychology as the science of self-reports and finger movements." *Perspectives on Psychological Science*, 2: pp.396-403. http://dx.doi.org/10.1111%2Fj.1745-6916.2007.00051.x (Accessed March 2013).

Bernays, E. (1955) *Engineering Consent*. Oklahoma: University of Oklahoma Press.

Bloemer, J.M.M. & H.D.P. Kasper. (1995) "The complex relationship between consumer satisfaction and brand loyalty." *Journal of Economic Psychology*, 16: pp.311-29.

Boym, S. (2010) *Another Freedom: The Alternative History of an Idea*. London: University of Chicago Press.

British Psychological Society (BPS). (2013) "The future of A-Level Psychology." Briefing paper. Leicester: BPS.

Brody, Y. (2014) "A Tortured Twist on Ethics." *Psychology Today*. http://www.psychologytoday.com/blog/limitless/201403/tortured-twist-ethics (Accessed March 2014).

Brysbaert, M. & K. Rastle. (2013) *Historical and Conceptual Issues in Psychology*. London: Pearson.

Chang, H-J. (2014) *Economics: The User's Guide*. London: Pelican.

Chomsky, N. (1967) "The Responsibility of Intellectuals." *New York Review of Books*. 23rd February.

http://www.nybooks.com/articles/archives/1967/feb/23/a-special-supplement-the-responsibility-of-intelle/ (Accessed Aug 2014).

—-. (2004) *Hegemony or Survival*. London: Penguin.

Cialdini, R. (2006) *The Psychology of Persuasion*. New York: Harper and Row.

Cialdini, R. & S. Cliffe. (2013) "The uses and abuses of influence." *Harvard Business Review*, 91 (7-8): pp.76-81.

Chartered Institute of Personnel and Development (CIPD). (2012) Research Report. *Where has all the trust gone?* London: CIPD.

Clare, A. (1980) *Psychiatry in Dissent* (2nd edition). London: Routledge.

Cohen, S. (2001) *States of Denial: Knowing About Atrocities and Suffering*. London: Polity Press.

Cosgrove, L., S. Krimsky, M. Vijayaraghavan & L. Schneider. (2006) "Financial ties between DSM-IV panel members and the pharmaceutical industry." *Psychotherapy and Psychosomatics*, 75: pp.154-60.

Cotter, L.H. (1967) "Operant conditioning in a Vietnamese mental hospital." *American Journal of Psychiatry*, 124: pp.23-8.

Cromby, J., D. Harper & P. Reavey (2013) *Psychology, Mental Health and Distress*. New York: Palgrave Macmillan.

Curtis, A. (Dir.) (1995) *The Living Dead* (TV series). London: BBC.

Dennett, D. (1992) *Darwin's Dangerous Idea*. Harmondsworth: Penguin.

De Vries, M.R. & E.K. Wijnans. (2013) "Personality and military service." In B.A. Moore & J.E. Barnett (eds.) *Military Psychologists' Desk Reference*. New York: Oxford University Press.

Dietz, T. (2011) "The art of influence." *Nature*, 479: p.176. 10th November.

Dimitrijevic, N. (2011) *Duty to Respond*. Budapest: CEU Press.

Fisher, M. (2009) *Capitalist Realism: Is There No Alternative?* Winchester: Zero Books.

—-. (2011) "The privatisation of stress."
http://www.newleftproject.org/index.php/site/article_
comments/the_privatisation_of_stress (Accessed July 2013).

Foxall, G.R., R.E. Goldsmith & S. Brown. (1998) *Consumer Psychology for Marketing*. London: International Thomson Business Press.

Freud, S. (2008) *The Future of an Illusion*. London: Penguin.

Fromm, E. (1942) *The Fear of Freedom*. London: Bloomsbury.

—-. (1973) *The Crisis of Psychoanalysis*. Harmondsworth: Penguin.

—-. (1977) *To Have or To Be*. London: Bloomsbury.

—-. (2011) *Marx's Concept of Man*. Mansfield Centre, CT: Martino Publishing.

Gee, T. (2011) *Counterpower: Making Change Happen*. Oxford: New Internationalist Publications Ltd.

Georges, P.M., A-S. Bayle-Tourtoulou & M. Badoc. (2013) *Neuromarketing in Action: How to Talk and Sell to the Brain*. London: Kogan Page.

Gergen, K.J. (1973). "Social psychology as history." *Journal of Personality and Social Psychology* 26: pp.309-20.

—-. (1992) "Toward a postmodern psychology." In S. Kvale (ed.) *Psychology and Postmodernism*. London: Sage.

Gittings, J. (1991) *Beyond the Gulf War: The Middle East and the New World Order*. London: CIIR.

Global Research. (2014) "What Exactly Are the Spy Agencies Doing with their Bag of Dirty Tricks?"
http://www.globalresearch.ca/what-exactly-are-the-spy-agencies-doing-with-their-bag-of-dirty-tricks/5391555?print=1 (Accessed July 2014).

Gogol, N. (2005) *The Diary of a Madman: The Government Inspector and Selected Stories*. London: Penguin Classics.

Greenberg, G. (2011) "Inside the battle to define mental illness." *Wired Magazine*
http://www.wired.com/magazine/2010/12/ff_dsmv
(Accessed January 2011).

Greenwald, G. (2014) "How Covert Agents Infiltrate the Internet to Manipulate, Deceive, and Destroy Reputations." *The//Intercept.* https://firstlook.org/theintercept/2014/02/24/jtrig-manipulation/ (Accessed March 2014).

Harper, D. (2007) "The complicity of psychology in the security state." In R. Roberts (ed.) *Just War: Psychology and Terrorism.* Ross-On-Wye: PCCS Books.

Haslam, S.A. & S.D. Reicher. (2012) "When prisoners take over the prison: A social psychology of resistance." *Personality & Social Psychology Review*, 16 (2): pp.154-79.

Hedges, C. (2002) *War is a Force that Gives Us Meaning.* New York: Anchor Books.

Hepburn, A. (2003) *An Introduction to Critical Social Psychology.* London: Sage.

Herman, E.S. & N. Chomsky (1994) *Manufacturing Consent: The Political Economy of the Mass Media.* London: Vintage.

Hopewell, C.A. (2013) "History of Military Psychology." In B.A. Moore & J.E. Barnett (eds.) *Military Psychologists' Desk Reference.* New York: Oxford University Press.

Insel, T. (2013) "Transforming diagnosis." http://www.nimh.nih.gov/about/director/2013/transforming-diagnosis.shtml (Accessed May 2013).

Itten, T & Roberts, R. (2014) *The New Politics of Experience and the Bitter Herbs.* Monmouth: PCCS Books.

Jahoda, M. (1966) Foreword. In R.D. Laing, H. Phillipson & A.R. Lee, *Interpersonal Perception.* London: Tavistock.

James, L.C. & L. Pulley. (2013) "Military psychologists' roles in interrogation." In B.A. Moore & J.E. Barnett (eds.) *Military Psychologists' Desk Reference.* New York: Oxford University Press.

Jaspal, R. & A. Coyle. (in press) "Threat, Victimhood and Peace: Debating the 2011 Palestinian UN State Membership Bid." *Digest of Middle East Studies.*

Jaspal, R. & B. Nerlich. (in press) "Fracking in the UK Press:

Threat Dynamics in an Unfolding Debate." *Public Understanding of Science*.

Jaspal, R., B. Nerlich & M. Cinnirella. (2014) "Human Responses to Climate Change: Social Representation, Identity and Socio-Psychological Action." *Environmental Communication: A Journal of Nature and Culture*. 8 (1): pp.110-30.

Joseph, J. (2004) *The Gene Illusion*. Ross-On-Wye: PCCS Books.

Kahneman, D. (2012) *Thinking, Fast and Slow*. London: Penguin.

Kelly, G.A. (1955) *The Psychology of Personal Constructs*. New York: W.W. Norton & Co.

—-. (1970) "The Psychology of the Unknown." In D. Bannister (ed.) *New Perspectives in Personal Construct Theory*. London: Academic Press.

Kirsch, I. (2009) *The Emperor's New Drugs. Exploding the Anti-Depressant Myth*. London: The Bodley Head.

Klein, N. (2010) *No Logo*. New York: Picador.

Kvale, S. (2003) *Psychology and Postmodernism*. London: Sage.

Laing, R.D. & A. Esterson. (1964) *Sanity, Madness and the Family*. London: Tavistock.

Lewis, D. (2013) *The Brain Sell: When Science Meets Shopping*. London: Nicholas Brealey.

Marx, K. (1852/2006) *The 18th Brumaire of Louis Bonaparte*. Maryland: Wildside Press.

—-. (1990) *Capital: Vol. 1*. London: Penguin.

Marx, K. & Engels, F. (1975) *Manifesto of the Communist Party*. Peking: Foreign Languages Press.

McCoy, A.W. (2006) *A Question of Torture: CIA Interrogation, from the Cold War to the War on Terror*. New York: Metropolitan Books.

Milgram, S. (1974) *Obedience to authority*. London: Tavistock.

Miller, G.A. (1966) *Psychology: The Science of Mental Life*. Harmondsworth: Penguin.

Moore, B.A. & J.E. Barnett (eds.). (2013) *Military Psychologists' Desk Reference*. New York: Oxford University Press.

Morgan, K.O. (2014) "Society: Still no such thing." Review of D. Marquand, "Mammon's Kingdom: An essay on Britain now." *The Independent*. 17th May.

Moncrieff, J. (2008) *The Myth of the Chemical Cure*. Houndmills: Palgrave.

Moscovici, S. & G. Duveen (eds.) (2000) *Social Representations: Explorations in Social Psychology*. Cambridge: Polity.

Nahai, N. (2012) *Webs of Influence: The Psychology of Persuasion*. Edinburgh Gate: Pearson Education.

Nerlich, B. & R. Jaspal. (in press) "Images of Extreme Weather: Symbolising Human Responses to Climate Change." *Science as Culture*.

Nietzsche, F. (2003) *Beyond Good and Evil*. London: Penguin.

Nitzan, J. & S. Bichler. (2006) "Capitalism and war." http://www.globalresearch.ca/capitalism-and-war/3890 (Accessed March 2014).

Nolan, C. (Dir.) (2005) *Batman Begins*. Warner Bros.

Ogden, J. (2003) "Some problems with social cognition models: A pragmatic and conceptual analysis." *Health Psychology*, 22 (4): pp.424–8.

Owen, D. (2008) *In Sickness and in Power: Illness in Heads of Government During the Last 100 Years*. London: Methuen.

Parker, I. (2007) *Revolution in Psychology*. London: Pluto Press.

Patel, N. (2007) "Torture, psychology and the 'War on Terror': A human rights framework." In R. Roberts (ed.) *Just War: Psychology and Terrorism*. Ross-On-Wye: PCCS Books.

Petit, P. (2002) *To Reach The Clouds*. London: Faber and Faber.

Physicians for Human Rights (PHR). (2010) Experiments in Torture. "Evidence of Human Subject Research and Experimentation in the 'Enhanced' Interrogation Program." http://www.heartlandalliance.org/kovler/publications/experiments-in-torture.pdf (Accessed August 2014).

Popper, K. (2002) *The Logic of Scientific Discovery*. London: Routledge Classics.

Rampton, S. & J. Stauber. (2003) *Weapons of Mass Deception: The Uses of Propaganda in Bush's War on Iraq*. London: Robinson.

Read, J. & J. Reynolds. (2000) *Speaking Our Minds: An Anthology*. Houndmills: Palgrave.

Read, K. (2004) "A history of madness." In J. Read, L.R. Mosher & R. Bentall (eds.) *Models of Madness*. London: Routledge.

Reich, W. (1946/75) *The Mass Psychology of Fascism*. London: Pelican.

Richards, G. (1994) "The social contexts of psychology." *The Psychologist*, 7 (10): pp.456-7.

—-. (2002) *Putting Psychology in its Place: A Critical Historical Overview* (2nd edition). New York: Routledge.

Roberts, R. (2007) "British psychology's response to the invasion and occupation of Iraq." In R. Roberts (ed.) *Just War: Psychology and Terrorism*. Ross-On-Wye: PCCS Books.

Rogers, C. (1961) *On Becoming a Person: A Therapist's View of Psychotherapy*. London: Constable.

Rose, S., R.C. Lewontin & L.J. Kamin. (1984) *Not in Our Genes*. Harmondsworth: Penguin.

Rose, H. (2001) "Colonising the social sciences." In H. Rose & S. Rose, *Alas Poor Darwin: Arguments Against Evolutionary Psychology*. London: Vintage.

Rubenstein, L.S. (2003) "The medical community's response to torture." *The Lancet*, 361: p.1556.

Sanders, T. (2008) *Paying for Pleasure: Men Who Buy Sex*. Cullompton: Willan Publishing.

Schmitt, B. (2012) "The consumer psychology of brands." *Journal of Consumer Psychology*, 22 (1): pp.7-17.

Sève, L. (1978) *Man in Marxist Theory and the Psychology of Personality*. Sussex: The Harvester Press.

Shakeshaft, N.G., M. Trzaskowski, A. McMillan, K. Rimfeld, E. Krapohl et al. (2013) "Strong Genetic Influence on a UK Nationwide Test of Educational Achievement at the End of Compulsory Education at Age 16." *PLoS ONE* 8 (12): e80341.

10.1371/journal.pone.0080341 (Accessed December 2013).

Shallice, T. (1972) "The Ulster depth interrogation techniques and their relation to sensory deprivation research." *Cognition*, 1: pp.385-405.

Sheldrake, R. (2012) *The Science Delusion*. London: Coronet.

Skinner, B.F. (2002) *Beyond Freedom and Dignity*. Indiana: Hackett Publishing Company.

Smail, D. (2005) *Power, Interests and Psychology*. Ross-On-Wye: PCCS Books.

Sparks, K. (2014) Review of D. Lewis, *The Brain Sell: When Science Meets Shopping*. London: Nicholas Brealey. *The Psychologist*, 27 (6): pp.460-61.

Szasz, T. (1983) *Ideology and Insanity: Essays on the Psychiatric Dehumanisation of Man*. London: Marion Boyars.

—-. (2007a) *The Medicalisation of Everyday Life*. New York: Syracuse University Press.

—-. (2007b) *Coercion as Cure: A Critical History of Psychiatry*. London: Transaction Publishers.

Thaler, R.H. & C.R. Sunstein. (2008) *Nudge*. London: Penguin.

Winters, J. (2011) *Oligarchy*. New York: Cambridge University Press.

Wintour, P. (2010) "David Cameron's 'nudge unit' aims to improve economic behaviour."
http://www.theguardian.com/society/2010/sep/09/cameron-nudge-unit-economic-behaviour (Accessed Feb 2014).

Contemporary culture has eliminated both the concept of the public and the figure of the intellectual. Former public spaces – both physical and cultural – are now either derelict or colonized by advertising. A cretinous anti-intellectualism presides, cheerled by expensively educated hacks in the pay of multinational corporations who reassure their bored readers that there is no need to rouse themselves from their interpassive stupor. The informal censorship internalized and propagated by the cultural workers of late capitalism generates a banal conformity that the propaganda chiefs of Stalinism could only ever have dreamt of imposing. Zer0 Books knows that another kind of discourse – intellectual without being academic, popular without being populist – is not only possible: it is already flourishing, in the regions beyond the striplit malls of so-called mass media and the neurotically bureaucratic halls of the academy. Zer0 is committed to the idea of publishing as a making public of the intellectual. It is convinced that in the unthinking, blandly consensual culture in which we live, critical and engaged theoretical reflection is more important than ever before.

9781782796541